AN ACTION A DAY

S0-BJA-819

AN ACTION
A DAY

keeps global capitalism away

MIKE HUDEMA

ILLUSTRATED BY JACOB ROLFE

Between the Lines
Toronto, Canada

An Action a Day

© 2004 by Mike Hudema

First published in Canada in 2004 by
Between the Lines
720 Bathurst Street, Suite #404
Toronto, Ontario M5S 2R4
1-800-718-7201
www.btlbooks.com

NOTICE TO READERS:
Some activities outlined in this book could, in certain circumstances, involve violations of federal criminal laws, provincial laws, or municipal bylaws, or expose activists to liability in civil actions. Readers are advised to seek legal advice before undertaking any activity that entails a risk of legal consequences. The publisher assumes no liability for the consequences of any activity undertaken by readers.

National Library of Canada Cataloguing in Publication

Hudema, Mike, 1976–
    An action a day : keeps global capitalism away / Mike Hudema ; illustrations by Jacob Rolfe.

ISBN 1-896357-90-3

    1. Social action. 2. Protest movements. I. Title.

HN17.5.H78 2004   361.2'3   C2004-901093-X

Cover and text design by Jennifer Tiberio
Front cover photograph by Joseph Tohill
Printed in Canada by union labour

Between the Lines gratefully acknowledges assistance for its publishing activities from the Canada Council for the Arts, the Ontario Arts Council, the Government of Ontario through the Ontario Book Publishers Tax Credit program and through the Ontario Book Initiative, and the Government of Canada through the Book Publishing Industry Development Program.

THE CANADA COUNCIL | LE CONSEIL DES ARTS
FOR THE ARTS | DU CANADA
SINCE 1957 | DEPUIS 1957

Canadä

ONTARIO ARTS COUNCIL
CONSEIL DES ARTS DE L'ONTARIO

This book is dedicated to Karena Munroe and Tooker Gomberg.

Karena, there is no way that this book would ever have been completed without you. Most of the actions in this book are a direct result of the work you have done or the directions in which you have pushed me.

Tooker, I can't even begin to say how much you have done to help this planet. I can only hope that people use this book with the same flair and passion that you brought to this world.

If not now, when? If not here, where? If not you, who?

Contents

Preface

WHAT YOU SEE BEFORE you in this book is a collection of actions performed over a period of several years in Alberta. The ideas are not mine; in some cases the basic ideas have been around for decades, if not a century or more (as in "boycotts," for instance); many are new twists on old themes, and in many cases in their present form they are creations of amazing political organizers in Edmonton, and especially the women among them. I simply had the time to collect the actions and write them down, and decided that it would be good for a man to do some secretarial work for a change.

The Edmonton groups involved in carrying out these and other actions are EARTh (Emergency Access Route Theatre), the T.W.A.T. (True Wimmin Against Totalitarianism) team, EcoCity, FUNK (Fighting Unaccountable Naughty Korporations), the University of Alberta Students' Union MAC (Mobilization and Action Committee), and SWAG (Student Worker Action Group). But the real credit for this book should go to a number of women who were instrumental in formulating, producing, directing, and carrying out many of the wonderful actions to be found in these pages.

Karena Munroe was the inspiration and driving force behind several of the actions. She was the director of EARTh, the main co-ordinator of FUNK, and one of the many incredible members of the T.W.A.T. team. Her brilliant mind, unswerving dedication, and ability to never back down from a fight or call sexism when she sees it should be a message to us all.

Sophie Ares-Pilon is another member of the T.W.A.T. team. As a member of FUNK she shouted (in both official languages) the Charter of Rights and Freedoms to rows of riot cops firing tear gas and rubber bullets in the streets of Quebec City. She is full of energy and lights up every room she enters.

Haley Dawn Nelson was a writer, director, and actor in EARTh. As a member of FUNK, she took to the streets as Mickey Mouse; she is an accomplished singer, writer, and mother.

Shannon Phillips, another member of FUNK, worked as the researcher at the University of Alberta Students' Union. It would not have been possible to put this book together without her. She pushed me to write it, edited my work, and contributed to its content, including the Introduction. I owe her a heavy debt, not only for her help with this project, but also for being my friend and showing me that there are several ways in which we need to fight—and for being someone who is engaged in those fights.

Amanda Crocker, from Between the Lines, helped out in a couple of ways. For one thing, she put together the section on resources that appears at the end of the book. For another, working with the people at the Catalyst Centre, Toronto, she also contributed the list of "Things to Think about and Discuss before Taking Action." I want to thank her and the Catalyst group—Matt Adams, Chris Cavanagh, Christine McKenzie, and Corvin Russell—for coming through in the crunch. Thank you as well to Jennifer Tiberio for the great design, Jacob Rolfe for his terrific illustrations, and Robert Clarke for his superb editing skills.

Ultimately, this book is dedicated to the work of all the activists who have come before and those who will come after. It is you who dare to stand against the storm and participate in the formation of a different vision. Whether you are a concerned parent fighting for funding, or an indigenous activist in Chiapas, my heart and thoughts are with you all.

Introduction

by Mike Hudema and Shannon Phillips

A DEMOCRATIC SOCIETY DOESN'T just condone political action. It demands it. And political action can take a variety of forms. It might simply be chalking a political message on the sidewalk. Then again it might be the tens of thousands of people who moved into Quebec City in April 2001 to protest the Summit of the Americas. It could be creating gigantic puppets for an MP's visit, or it could be a roadside blockade. Political action includes Greenpeace militants climbing to the top of a building to drop a banner. It could include a pensioner in a tiny one-bedroom apartment writing a letter to her local MP; or someone writing a critical letter to the editor of the local newspaper. It will almost certainly be actions that have not yet been dreamed of, that we can now only imagine.

This book draws together a mix of some of the most successful and doable actions taken over recent years—from our fun number 1, "Radical Cheerleading," to our very serious number 52, "Blockades." The book is aimed at activists, or budding activists, and people who simply want to know what it is that is happening out there on the streets— but it is definitely not meant to be all things to all people. For example, it will not give you a guide to how to incorporate yourself as a society or how to write for grants—two things that will put you on the road to long-term funding and organizing. The book will not give you tidbits of research for your pamphlet or even a framework of analysis—this you can develop on your own time. Above all, *the book is by no means intended to replace all the vital and hard work and thought that goes into political action on an everyday basis*—all the ongoing work that is required to really make a difference in the world. What it does, we believe, is simply add another tool to the activist's toolbox.

It also does not (and here we hope we won't be accused of false advertising) actually contain an action a day. That sounds good, and we wanted it for our title, but all we could pack into this book was an action a week, and we think you will agree that an action a week is more than enough for now. It's easy enough, after all, to fill up the days of the week organizing and planning for one action.

INTRODUCTION

The actions that follow are heavy on drama, theatre, and media-friendly visuals. They are meant to inspire you to act, and to give you ideas for work you can do in your own community. They are also meant to provoke thought about what is possible. As activists we have a lot of tools, and this book will, we hope, indicate just how vast your toolbox really is. Many of the actions incorporate a letter or a petition (those two bastions of what often seems to be political futility), but then again the political act is not in signing a letter or a petition, but in how the ideas are presented.

This book is aimed at people who are at least a little curious about ways of taking steps, however small, towards making this world a better place for future generations—indeed, make sure there is a world for future generations. And it's for people who want to have a certain amount of fun, and some immediate satisfaction, in working towards that lofty, seemingly distant goal.

Do not use this book with caution. Take one of these ideas and run with it—adapt it however you want, get it done—and enjoy the feeling that, if only for a few minutes, or a few hours, you have truly worked to make change in the world.

Things to Think about and Discuss before Taking Action

What are the objectives of your action?

Getting media attention? Disrupting a meeting or event? Livening up some public space? Reviving yourself or other activists? Building community? Changing legislation? Creating alternative structures?

Will the action you have planned achieve these objectives?

How does this action fit into a larger campaign?

Are there other groups that could provide more long-term support for the action?

What action suits your objectives the best?

Lobbying? Letter writing? Rallies? Occupations? Media stunts? Petitions? Educational workshops? Writing books or zines? Or something else?

How will you communicate with your audience?

Will you engage with hecklers or ignore them?

What will you say to the media?

Will you prepare talking points?

Who, if anyone, will speak on behalf of your group?

Do you have gender parity?

Does your action communicate, both verbally and visually, the message you want to convey?

What are the possible consequences of your action? (intended or unintended, good or bad)

What are the possible consequences for members of your group?

What are the consequences for your audience or others around you?

How will the media spin your action?

Have you prepared for these consequences?

Are there any health or safety concerns you need to prepare for?

Are you prepared for any legal consequences that might arise from your action? At what point will you call it off?

How will you react if security or the police show up?

Will one member of the group act as a liaison?

Do you have legal support in case you need it?

How will you defuse a tense situation?

Is your message more important than your action or are you committed to the action for its own sake?

If you decide to change tactics or end the action, how will you do this?

THINGS TO THINK ABOUT

How will your group make decisions before, during, and after your action?

By consensus? Majority rules? With one all-powerful dictator?
Do you ensure equal participation from traditionally marginalized groups within your actions?

Gandhi said, "We must be the change we wish to see." Will your group's method of making decisions reflect your own values and ideals?

Check out the web resources listed at the back of this book for more information on planning safe, effective actions and organizing fun groups that allow everyone to participate.

After the Action

Sometime after the action you might want to get together and talk about how the action went.

What went well?
What would you do differently next time?
Was your action politically effective?

Use this information to make your next action even better.

Radical Cheerleading

FUN 🏃🏃🏃🏃½ | RISK ⚠ | RESOURCES ☛

THIS ACTION IS fairly easy. All it takes is a few dedicated individuals and a lot of enthusiasm. My first experience with radical cheerleading was in Edmonton at a protest against Bill 11, a controversial health-care bill that allows private, for-profit hospitals in Alberta. At the top of the steps of the Alberta Legislature stood eight stunningly clad cheerleaders, four men and four women. Each cheerleader was dressed in a red or black shirt and a skirt of the opposite colour, and held the traditional pom poms (red and black). They began by standing in a line with their backs to the crowd, their arms straight out to the side. Then the call went out: "Radical cheerleaders ready?" And the reply "FUNK YAH!!" Then the cheers began, accompanied by pom pom waving and cartwheels, somersaults, and log rolls.

The cheerleaders whipped the crowd into a frenzy. The cheers were done in regular cheerleading fashion, but with funky movements all of their own. They included chants and repeats to get audience participation. All the cheers focused on a particular issue.

WHY RADICAL CHEERLEADING?

Radical cheerleading is a way of providing effective social commentary in a way that is engaging and does not alienate people. The action has the ability to entertain both the audience and the participants—it is truly fun. The smiles that come from the participants and the crowd are pretty amazing. Often, when people hear chanting they may stop for a second or two to watch and listen, but our experience with radical cheerleading is that onlookers will stay for cheer after cheer.

In addition to their entertainment and motivational values, radical cheerleaders can also serve as a de-escalation tool for tense situations. This concept was never entirely clear to me until I was part of the cheerleaders in a march against the annual meeting of the World Petroleum Congress, a coalition of the world's oil giants, in Calgary. After events like the 1999 WTO meetings in Seattle, the police in Calgary were fully equipped and ready for anything. But this time, whenever a verbal battle between demonstrators and police erupted—with the potential of ending in tear gas and pepper spray—the radical cheerleaders were among the groups that helped to defuse the situation. The men and women in skirts, through their witty cheering and funky choreography, were able to inject enough humour and fun into the march to relieve the tension. It is difficult for police to contemplate pepper spraying cheerleaders. The cheerleaders—along with some amazing theatre and speeches—helped to get the message out to the public, while at the same time exposing the police state that had been set in place to deal with a small group of non-violent protesters.

At one point, while waiting by our van, we were asked by two police officers to perform some of our cheers. We gave them a few chants, were able to give them additional information on the World Petroleum Congress, and even got to do our cheers while they put the siren lights on.

WHAT YOU NEED

All you need is a group of dedicated individuals, uniforms, and cheers. Men and women in skirts dress in matching uniforms—so you will need black or red tops and the alternate colour skirt, a pair of combat boots, some red and black pompoms, and a lot of charisma and funky moves. Then you need cheers. As a starting point see the cheers here, lifted from the work of the Edmonton Radical Cheerleaders. But you can, of course, make up your own: start with your favourite kid's song, perhaps, and go from there. Work in lines about the issue you are focusing on. The choreography takes time, but working on it can be a blast. Try doing it in collaboration with a potluck or wine and cheese party.

Plan around your issue and decide where you want to perform. Remember to smile: you are the energy of the crowd—if you are low, others will be low too, but if you are in high spirits, you will have a political singalong on your hands before you know it.

There are a couple of radical cheerleaders websites, with lots more information, and cheers. See ‹www.geocities.com/radicalcheerleaders› or ‹http://radcheers.tripod.com/RC›.

RADICAL CHEERS

1

[patty cake]
End the Use of Oil
In cars and in our homes
There's smarter ways of doing things
Than burning dino...

Bones are in the closet
The PR men can't hide
We're fucking up the atmosphere
And committing geno...

Side deals in the backroom
Politicians on the take
If we keep burning fossil fuels
Our atmosphere will...

Baking on the beaches
Cancer's on the rise
We've got to wake the people up
And make them real...

Eyes are on the future
On solar we'll depend
We'll stop the use of fossil fuels
And the oil age will...
(Repeat)

2

Solar and wind are safe and clean
Let's shut down the oil machine
We are here to let you know
The time has come for oil to go
You can't take us for a ride
You must stop the genocide
Even though you think we're small
United we will make you fall!

3

To the left
To the left
Not to the right to the left
My back is aching
My skirt's too tight
My booty's shaking
From the left to the right
Shout it out
Shout it out
REVOLUTION
REVOLUTION
Acka backa you're a soda cracker
Your jobs, your money, your institution
That never listen to the people's needs
It's all about greed
It's all about greed
BEEP BEEP BEEP
Take your voice to the street
Enough is enough
It's time to rise up
The rich get richer
While the earth gets sicker
So kiss the back of my butt
Kiss the back of my butt

Kiss the back of my
Kiss the back of my
Kiss the back of my butt!

4

There was a company whose name was Shell
And climate change was its game-o
S - H - E - L - L [x 3]
And climate change was its game-o
There was a company named Esso
And pollution was its game-o
[Clap] E - S - S - O [x 3]
And pollution was its game-o
There was a company named Oxy
And genocide was its game-o
[Clap - Clap] O - X - Y [x 3]
And genocide was its game-o
There was a company named BP
And PR was its game-o
[Clap - Clap - Clap] B - P [x 3]
And PR was its game-o
There is a person who really cares
And you can make a change-o
[Clap - Clap - Clap - Clap] YOU! [x 3]
And you can make a change-o.

THINK OF THE BUSIEST street you know and imagine someone lying in the middle of the sidewalk—motionless and pointing to something ahead of them that is only vaguely apparent. You walk along, seeing person after person, each motionless. You hurry on until eventually you come to the end of the line, and discover the secret.

This action was suggested to me by one of my friends after she had watched a Radiohead video. In the video a man is lying down in the middle of the sidewalk, unable to move because of a secret he possesses. The secret is so powerful that if he says it out loud, it will paralyze anyone in earshot into the same motionless position.

The action involves several individuals— from four to five is a good number. Each of them becomes "a station" in a continuing line of bodies. They lie down in the middle of a busy sidewalk, about fifteen to twenty metres apart— close enough so that the next participant is visible, but far enough away that pedestrians are intrigued enough to follow on to the next station (person). Each person is flat against the pavement, with one arm stretched out and index finger pointing to the next station. Ideally, the last person's body will be kind of curved around a corner, so that at first the pedestrians can't see the final image and have to go around the corner before they find out what it is.

The final image, or message, can be whatever best serves your action. One possibility is a sign that introduces, or outlines, the issue you are trying to raise around this action. You might have a petition for people to sign. The sign might say, for instance: if you've come this far, how about taking one more small step—please sign our petition.

The final piece of the puzzle is up to you, but remember to keep it simple enough so that your audience will clearly understand why your burden is so great that you and the others have been forced down to the pavement. You may also want to put a different word on each person: as people walk along they will be further intrigued by each person, and eventually come to your final message.

WHY RADIOHEAD?

This action works on two levels: it can help you get your message out, and it is so easy and straightforward to do that it can instil confidence in your group.

The action engages your audience. People can't help but stop and wonder about what's going on. It is creative and it gives the passersby something to talk about later as they go through their day—even if it's a statement like, "These crazy idiots were lying in the middle of the sidewalk protesting car pollution." The action starts a much-needed dialogue. It breaks people out of their daily routines and gets them thinking.

Doing actions like this one can also help to make a group more confident—and confidence is important for other actions that require people to engage with news reporters, politicians, or police officers. Radiohead provides a good start at building confidence, because all it requires in terms of commitment is for participants to lie on the ground and not move. Do the action for an hour or so, then retreat to your local coffee shop and debrief. Watch as this action helps bring the group together.

WHAT YOU NEED

All you need—in addition to an issue that needs to be addressed—is a group of four to five people willing to lie down on a sidewalk, plus a busy location and a final image. This is one of the great parts about this action—it doesn't require a lot of materials or preparation to make it successful.

Try it. It may sound weird but it can be highly effective.

ACTION ③ Sidewalk–Chalking

| FUN ✤✤✤✤ | RiSK ½ | RESOURCES ½ |

CHALKING IS AN action inspired by all the children who have ever taken freedom of expression into their own hands and drawn on a sidewalk. Our version comes out of the experience of Emergency Access Route Theatre (EARTh), a troupe in Edmonton that does interactive theatre focused on social issues. It does performances for high-school and community groups, but also carries out a lot of theatre actions in the street.

One day during a scheduled EARTh rehearsal, actors got talking about the number of billboards they were seeing all around them— about how the content was almost unavoidable and how it was shaping people's lives for the worst. The group's members decided to take the day off from rehearsing. They picked up a bucket of sidewalk chalk and headed downtown to the heart of the city to create their own billboards. With six people chalking at the same time, within a matter of minutes the group had covered an entire section of sidewalk with political messages, from "Read Chomsky" to "Take back our world" to "Plant a tree here." My favourite was "You can change the world," with arrows drawn from the message to pedestrians standing on the street. The group spent an hour and a half working on five city blocks.

Later, as they retraced their route, they were absolutely amazed by the number of people who were stopping to read the messages. People simply couldn't ignore them. EARTh had also left some pieces of chalk along the way, so that people could write their own messages, and many passersby took up the challenge.

WHY SIDEWALK-CHALKING?

Sidewalks are one of the few free spaces left where we can legally express ourselves. The sidewalk is a canvas, and when something is written on it, people will stop to read the message—sometimes to the extent of creating small pedestrian traffic jams.

You can use chalk to engage people in thought—give them something to think about. You can encourage passersby to take part by offering them pieces of chalk.

Sidewalk chalking is also empowering: people get a safe space and an environment they can use to deliver a message to the world. By chalking you highlight the sheer amount of commodified, privatized space there is, and you also get your group's message out, whatever it may be.

Sidewalk chalking can also be a great way of promoting events. Poster boards or lampposts often become plastered with material promoting everything under the sun. Sidewalks are free, and no one will poster over you.

WHAT YOU NEED

All you need is a bucket of thick, sturdy, colourful chalk and a group of people ready and willing to express themselves freely. You can chart out what you want to do or say beforehand, link a message to an issue, or simply write and draw as inspiration comes to you. You can concentrate your messages or space them out, even take over entire city blocks with chalk.

Just pick a busy location and get to work.

THE WORD "SOAPBOX," as in "get on your soapbox," has been traced back to 1907. One dictionary defines it as "an improvised platform used by a self-appointed, spontaneous or informal orator; broadly: something that provides an outlet for delivering opinions." In the earlier years the actual soapbox was usually a rough wooden box, or any raised temporary platform used by the people making their speeches. Today people speaking their minds tend not to use boxes—and if they stand on anything, it is just as likely to be a plastic milk crate—but the expression remains. As Evan Morris, "The Word Detective," puts it, "Many people would argue that more truth has been spoken from soap boxes than we'll ever hear on TV."

Unfortunately, as public spaces are encroached upon, and as we look to media rather than ourselves for the expression of ideas, soapboxing has fallen by the wayside, which is a shame. The theatre troupe EARTh accidentally brought soapboxing back to the forefront when one of our rehearsals was cancelled. We decided that instead of making the day a complete write-off we would practise speaking in front of an audience. We reclaimed a crate from the local liquor store, went downtown, stood on the box, and started ranting.

Downtown also offers a great muse—filled as it is with billboards, Starbucks coffee shops, corporate CEO head-quarters, and, on a busy day, a captive audience. We were a little shaky at first. We would walk a block, put our box down, and speak whatever was on our minds. It is hard at first, but after a while the words just seem to roll out. You get a strong sense of empowerment when you put into words, in public, your thoughts and knowledge about the issue that's on your mind.

That first day we ended our action in the middle of a fountain at City Hall in Edmonton. We invited anyone who was interested to come up and participate. The highlight of the action came when a twelve-year-old girl waded across the pool and told the audience why they too must speak out. On a cloudy summer day a dozen or so people we didn't know took up the young girl's challenge and ranted on everything from the weather to the lack of low-income housing.

WHY SOAPBOXING?

Soapboxing is an action that can start a much-needed conversation. Most of us only gripe about our world in the confines of our homes, to people who already know about the issues. Soapboxing brings those conversations into a public forum. As more and more of our space is commodified and privatized, we need to reclaim and build spaces where ordinary people can express their ideas.

Soapboxing is not only good for democracy, but also liberating for the speaker. There is nothing like a good rant in the open air to get your heart pumping and that issue off your chest and into action.

WHAT YOU NEED

All you need is a sturdy crate of some sort. Then just add a few people and find a place to jump on your soapbox. This is an action anyone can do—encourage members of your audience to come up and have their say. I like to keep my rants positive and try to empower the people around me, but a good gripe works too. You can plan your speeches in advance or improvise them—the objective is to get your voice out there.

If you want more security, bring some friends along. It is great to have a crowd, but especially great to have the makings of a friendly one, and if you can bring your own along, that is one less thing you have to worry about. It also means there are other people around who might want to join in. Most people find it hard to be the first person to stop and listen, but add a few people (your friends) and passersby may notice the welcoming environment.

What Will You Work For?

FUN ✂✂✂   RISK ½   RESOURCES ☂

I BORROWED THIS action from a cartoon I saw in a book on direct action. It is my hope that whoever drew the cartoon will realize that we are all working in solidarity, and will not sue me for what little money I have.

The action works as follows: one person gets dressed up in what is her or his oldest, most worn, everyday clothes—something that can represent what a homeless person might wear. Another person dresses in a business suit and carries a briefcase. The two of them stand about twenty feet apart on a busy city street, close to a wall in front of a bank. Each holds a cardboard sign. The sign held by the homeless person says, "Will work for food." The sign the business person carries says, "Will work for $500,000 a year, plus dental and health benefits, company car, paid vacations, demands continued on back."

The action is simple: two people standing silently, holding signs, periodically eyeing one another. As the action wears on, they progressively give each other longer stares, and begin uncomfortably shifting back and forth as they eye one another. Performing this action when issues of affordable housing and/or homelessness have been in the news can help to crystallize problems that need to be addressed.

WHY WHAT WILL YOU WORK FOR?

First, this action is quite straightforward and easy to do. Second, our world is full of contradictions, and these contradictions need to be exposed. This action is a visual representation of the gap between rich and poor.

WHAT YOU NEED

Two signs: one saying "Will work for food" and the other one saying "Will work for $500,000 a year" and all the rest. Then you need the appropriate clothes, and two individuals willing to stand on the street and perform.

ACTION **6** *Corporate Welfare*

FUN ⚒⚒⚒ | RISK ½ | RESOURCES 🛠

THIS ACTION IS almost identical to Action 5, but with a slightly different message. A small group of us performed it for the Alberta provincial election.

Again, one person dresses up as someone who would be stereotypically recognized as being homeless. The other person dresses in a business suit and carries a brief case. Both actors stand about twenty feet apart, and each of them holds a cardboard sign. The sign being held by the homeless person gives the dollar figure for the total amount of social assistance that a single person receives under your jurisdiction's welfare policy, and the sign held by the businessperson indicates the amount of corporate "subsidies" given out, directly or indirectly, by whatever government is being targeted.

The action is simply two people standing silently, close to a wall on a busy street, holding signs, each of them keeping a wary eye on the other every once in a while.

WHY CORPORATE WELFARE?

This action can highlight a particular sector of industry. For example, the oil and gas industry weasels its way out of hundreds of millions in royalty payments every year, and that's something that needs to be exposed. Also, the public's perception of "welfare" is often unfavourable. A common perception is that people on social assistance are lazy bums who suck money out of the system or, even worse, cheat to get their hands on the taxpayer's hard-earned cash. What needs to be emphasized is that the ones who are really cheating, who are really sucking the money out of the system, are corporations, which typically receive far more federal and provincial welfare funds than people on social assistance could ever dream of seeing. Instead of being labelled as "welfare," corporate handouts are cleverly hidden behind the more acceptable terms of "subsidy" or "tax break."

This action seeks to break down those distinctions, expose the real abusers of the system, and help people start pointing fingers in the right direction.

WHAT YOU NEED

Two signs, a homeless outfit, a business suit, and two individuals to stand on the street.

ACTION 7

The Buddha Walk

FUN 🏃🏃🏃🏃½ | RISK ⚠️⚠️½ | RESOURCES ½

THIS ACTION HAS its origins in the documentary movie *Baraka* (1992) — in the scene where a monk is moving ever so slowly and peacefully through a busy city street. EARTh took that idea and adapted it one day in a large shopping mall.

Four of us started moving in *super slow motion*, all in a straight line, one behind the other, as the busy mall patrons passed us by. The action worked—shopper after shopper stopped to watch as we made our way from the ground floor to the main floor. As people gathered, many of them wondered out loud about what we were doing and why we were there. Some of them thought we were part of the Fringe, an annual theatre festival in Edmonton. Others remarked that we were simply strange, and one person suggested that we were going to steal something.

All of these conversations happened within earshot, as if folks believed that because we were moving slowly we couldn't hear what they were saying. Eventually a mall security officer arrived and engaged us in conversation as we continued our slow progression through the mall.

Security: You have to stop that or I'll have to remove you.

Us: Stop what?

Security: What you are doing.

Us: What are we doing?

Security: You are creating a spectacle.

Us: How are we creating a spectacle?

Security: Well . . . uh . . . you are walking slowly.

Us: Yes, we are walking slowly.

Security: Well, you can't. You can't walk slowly in here.

Us: We can't walk slowly?

Security: No.

Us: [pointing to an elderly person moving across the mall very slowly] Well, what about her? She's moving very slowly.

Security: No, she's moving at the appropriate speed—you are moving too slowly.

Us: Can you show me what is the appropriate speed? I mean how slowly can we walk and still remain in the mall?

Security: [getting flustered] No, you simply have to leave the mall. Leave the mall or I will call the police to remove you.

At that point, we left the mall. We didn't feel the need to press the issue with the police department. But as we walked off a very strange thing happened. The crowd that had gathered started clapping for us and jeering at the security officials. These shoppers—primarily middle-aged people—were now clapping, partly because of the absurdity of the situation and partly, perhaps, because we all have a desire to stand up to authority and we get a certain sense of catharsis when we see other people doing that.

This is one of the best actions for a lazy day when you want just a little something to do.

WHY THE BUDDHA WALK?

This is an excellent way of getting people to think about the pace of our lives. The contrast between you and your audience is truly amazing, and passersby find your slow procession fascinating to watch. Be prepared to get lots of people watching and asking questions. You can ignore the questions and have the audience derive their own meanings, or you can have handbills or a sign outlining your intentions.

We live in a time when we all seem to be out of breath most of the time, running from place to place. This action lets *you* take a much-needed breath. At the same time, the action breaks people out of their routines, which is one of the first steps to change.

Our society works on a set of rules that we don't recognize very often. It seems that we have set ways of doing things, and if we don't do things in those ways we are cast as weirdos or crazy. People who have travelled to other countries know what I am trying to get at all too well. Most of our ideas are confined to what we know, and it is only when we see other ways of being and knowing that we can start to think about which of our internalized codes of behaviour are reasonable, and which ones are only there to oppress us. When we travel, we see new realities and different ways in which society can work.

This action breaks down those internalized rules and calls acceptable behaviour into question—and you and/or your audience don't even have to travel to faraway lands to achieve that.

WHAT YOU NEED

All you need is a group of people who can walk slowly—and the slower the better. You can also add props or costumes. One day we used a box with the word "consumer" written on all of its sides, and went slow-motion shopping. When we walked along the mall corridors we moved in slow motion, and when we went through stores we moved in fast-forward.

This action works well with no props at all, so anything you add is just icing on the cake. This is the easiest action in the book.

THE CRITICAL MASS IS one of my favourite actions. The critical mass movement is based on the act of bicycles taking back the street. Instead of cyclists being squished to the side of the road, in this case dozens, hundreds, or even thousands of bicycles take up every lane of traffic and have a safe ride from one location to another. This action has been used around the world and is an easy way to start community conversations about car pollution, public space, and alternative forms of transportation, or just to improve bike safety.

Starting at an agreed upon location, cyclists take to the street, riding en masse along a previously designated route. Some cyclists ride ahead to block traffic at streetlights, and to make sure that the group stays together. Others ride around handing out pamphlets explaining the action, but most of the cyclists just ride.

In Edmonton critical mass rides began in the early 1990s. In recent years the numbers of participants were waning a little, and something needed to change. In 2003 that something turned out to be the introduction of theme rides, which are just like theme or costume parties, except on bicycles. We had a different theme every month, with the highlights being the Halloween and Santa Claus rides—even though the temperature at Christmas time was minus-thirty degrees. Just picture fifty Santas riding down the busiest street in your town or city.

Critical mass rides have been done in many cities, so check around to make sure you are not duplicating work. If there is no critical mass ride in your town, then get it going. You'll be amazed at how many zany

bike-related ideas pop up after a ride. For example, one bike activist hooks his bike up to a small electrical generator connected to a blender to make bicycle-powered smoothies at the end of every ride.

WHY CRITICAL MASS?

These days safely riding a bike down a busy road is next to impossible. Most streets don't have bike lanes, and cyclists find themselves forced to ride dangerously close to the side of the road as cars continuously whip by and cut them off. Many cyclists ride illegally on the sidewalks because of how dangerous it is to be on the road.

Our entire lives seem to revolve around the automobile. Instead of planning for sustainable alternatives, most cities are completely automobile-centric. Critical mass is an opportunity for the cyclists of the world to take to the streets and see what a car-free world would be like.

This event is as empowering as it is fun. Being able to take over the streets and ride with others in complete safety produces a truly magical feeling. Critical mass rides also build community—a community of people who believe in the values of sustainable energy—a benefit that is truly priceless.

WHAT YOU NEED

With any action of this sort, you need outreach. For critical mass, you need first of all to make sure that people come out to the ride—and so you need to do intensive postering, use listserves (a list of e-mail addresses maintained on a computer that distributes messages among a group of recipients), make announcements at other events, and use the media. Then you need to explain the action to the people around you as you ride. Handbills are a good idea, as motorists are likely to get pretty peeved if you don't tell them what you are doing and why. Giving them a handbill can help take some of the car angst away and ensure a safer ride for everyone. Information materials can be downloaded off the critical mass website, or you can make up your own.

Local bike shops are among the best places to gain support for critical mass. They will probably put up your poster or otherwise help you publicize the event. This will help you get the message out beyond the cadre of activists to a wider bicycle-friendly audience—people who are not necessarily politicized but are nonetheless willing to help out.

After you have your outreach materials it's just a matter of picking a time, a starting point, a route, and a finishing point. The last Friday of every month at 5:00 p.m. is the time for several critical mass rides across Canada. That time of day allows people who work to attend, and Friday is a good day to relax or let loose. It's good when choosing your route to take into account flow of traffic, accessibility, traffic lights, one- way streets, or any other hazards. Once you have your route chosen, appoint a few route marshals to block traffic at intersections and keep people safe. This is especially important during your first few rides, when every-one is new to the experience.

After you have done a few rides, people will fall into whatever roles they feel comfortable with, and marshals will emerge. Before your first ride, travel along the route once with a couple of friends just to make sure you didn't overlook anything. Add twenty to twenty thousand cyclists and you are ready to roll.

ACTION 9

Reclaim the Streets

FUN ❄❄❄❄½ | RISK ⚠⚠⚠⚠ | RESOURCES ☞☞☞☞☞

STREET RECLAMATION has been practised for years and has taken place on several different continents. It has enabled people to reclaim their power in a world that, it seems, has largely taken that power away. It's based on the principle that power, as a radical website puts it, fears cel-ebration.

The event takes a lot of organization and calls for a certain amount of leg- and brain-work, but it really gets the juices flowing and can be a lot of fun to get started.

The first reclaim the streets action in Edmonton happened in 1998. The action coincided with two strategic happenings in the city: the Fringe, a theatre festival, and the critical mass event (see Action 8). The reclamation planning took months of effort and dedication: surveying the area, deciding on a reclamation site, finding the equipment, dealing with logistics, organizing volunteers. We spread the word with leaflets asking people to meet at a certain location—though the place we named was not the site to be reclaimed, which was on the fringe of the Fringe Festival area and at the finish point of the critical mass cycling event. The police may take an interest in your event, but if your meeting place is different from your reclaimed space, they won't be able to shut you down immediately.

In our case, we met at a local school, three blocks away from the target location. Participants brought skipping ropes, sidewalk chalk, and puppets. The Fringe already had barriers set up, so that all we needed to do was slightly alter those already existing traffic barricades to create our own space. And we added a barrier made out of skipping ropes delivered by the critical mass riders. A bus equipped with a turntable was already parked in the street—we kept the parking meters filled with coins throughout the day.

At 4:00 p.m., all of the groups converged; the group from the school, the critical mass riders, a barricade patrol, and the party security. The barricade patrol used the existing barricades to block off the south exits, the critical mass blocked off the north, the turntable was unveiled, and a DJ started busting tunes as the street flooded with people. All of this happened in about five minutes. Being close to the Fringe festival meant that we had an already-established party atmosphere to work with. Lots of people joined in. Some of them thought that our event was simply an extension of the Fringe.

The police arrived in thirty minutes, but by that time they were unable or unwilling to do anything about our action because a) there were too many people, and b) people thought it was a Fringe event and any police interference itself would seem to be a disruption. Although the police didn't like it, they let the event continue and diverted traffic around the party. The event concluded at 8:00, and two people were eventually arrested.

WHY RECLAIM THE STREETS?

I think I can best explain this by offering two quotes from a "Reclaim the Streets" (RTS) website <www.reclaimthestreets.net>.

The privatization of public space in the form of the car continues the erosion of neighbourhood and community that defines the metropolis. Road schemes, business "parks," shopping developments—all add to the disintegration of community and the flattening of a locality.

Everywhere becomes the same as everywhere else. Community becomes commodity—a shopping village, sedated and under constant surveillance. The desire for community is then fulfilled elsewhere, through spectacle, sold to us in simulated form. A TV soap "street" or "square" mimicking the arena that concrete and capitalism are destroying. The real street, in this scenario, is sterile. A place to move through, not to be in. It exists only as an aid to somewhere else - through a shop window, billboard or petrol tank.

RTS is a stand against this erosion of public space, for it is:

ultimately in the *streets* that power must be dissolved: for the *streets* where daily life is endured, suffered and eroded, and where power is confronted and fought, must be turned into the domain where daily life is *enjoyed, created and nourished.*

A street party demonstrates how we can make our own fun without asking permission. For a few hours the longing for free space is not simply an unfulfilled dream about escape, but the transformation of the here and now.

(For another type of reclaim the streets action, see Action 39.)

WHAT YOU NEED

Drums, costumes, whistles, bells, juggling balls, beach balls, skipping ropes, dancing shoes, poetry, bubbles, and hugs; but no drugs or thugs. You also need to select a location that is both accessible to the public and somewhere you can easily block off for a period of time. The location is usually kept secret, so you also need an alternate location where people can initially meet and then move from there to the convergence space. You need to organize how you are going to block everything off and also determine roles for your group—media and police liaisons, people to block the road, and peace police to maintain tranquillity. One word of caution: the organizers are legally liable for any damage caused during the event, which means that you should plan how to keep the identities of the organizers a secret. For more information, check out a truly wonderful website: **<www.reclaimthestreets.net>**.

10 ACTION *Information Booth*

FUN ✱✱✱ | RISK ⚠⚠½ | RESOURCES ✱✱✱

MY FRIEND KARENA MUNROE came up with this idea when we were at a folk festival. We were getting a little tired from all the activity, and Karena suggested that we go sit and relax at an abandoned information booth. We sat down behind the booth's counter and started talking, but before very long people started coming up to us and asking for directions to the various events and stages of the festival. They all seemed to assume that we had the information they required.

So, we decided, why not set up our own information booth? And that became the impetus for this action. Build a structure, put an information sign on it, and get ready to give information—*your* information. When someone comes up to you and asks for directions, or whatever, before directing them on their journey tell them a little about the situation in Sierra Leone or the problems the Lubicon Cree are facing—or whatever issues you are working on. You may even have a petition or letter for them to sign.

WHY INFORMATION BOOTH?

An information booth is culturally recognized as a place where it is okay to ask questions. We all have information that we want to get out into the world, and this action allows you to dispense it to people who come to you for advice. They can take it or leave it, as they wish, but at least you've had a chance to offer it.

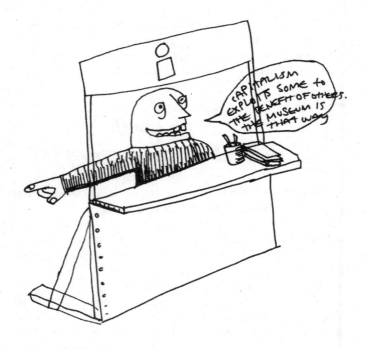

WHAT YOU NEED

The first thing you need is a booth. Any kind of makeshift structure will do, but the closer you can get to the actual thing, the better. If people see your venue as a "real" information booth, then more of them will approach you. You can get wood by Dumpster diving and find the rest of the stuff you need by other means of foraging or by borrowing or even (horrors) buying it. Of course, you also need the information you want to dispense; and you may want to have letters or petitions for people to sign so that they can take action on the information.

Check out the legal implications around the placement of your booth. Private property is out, but most public sites should be fair game. Co-ordinating your booth with a sporting event, festival, or a fair will add to your credibility and increase numbers.

Voicing Homelessness

ACTION 11

FUN 🏃🏃🏃 | RISK ⚠️⚠️½ | RESOURCES 🕯️🕯️🕯️

CHOOSE ONE PERSON to dress up as a stereotypical homeless panhandler. Your "panhandler" sits on a busy street and puts a hat out, as if begging for change. As she or he sits there, a nearby participant, hidden from view as much as possible, plays a tape of recorded voices expressing various (objectionable and pejorative) typical thoughts or stereotypes that people associate with panhandling or homelessness: you're a drunk, a bum, take a bath, get a job, get out of town—that sort of thing.

You play the tape loud enough for people walking by to hear, but not so loud that it overwhelms the effectiveness of the action. With the tape concealed, pedestrians are confronted with both the sight of the "panhandler" and the conflicting sounds.

WHY VOICING HOMELESSNESS?

This action makes explicit stereotypes regarding homelessness and poverty. It brings prejudices to the surface and forces a confrontation with our inner selves. This action refuses to let people simply pass a homeless person by, pretending that person doesn't exist. Instead, the action speaks out common inner thoughts and makes people deal with them. The idea is that we all need to realize our connection to each other, and that anyone's suffering is our suffering.

Sufi interruption. One day a man walked to a friend's house and knocked on the door. "Who's there?" his friend asked. "It's me," the man replied. "Well then, I cannot let you in, for there is already too much distance between us." After wandering the countryside for three years, wondering what his friend meant, the man went back and knocked on his friend's door once again. "Who's there?" asked the friend. "It's you," the man answered. The friend opened the door.

WHAT YOU NEED

You need a stereotypical "homeless" outfit and a person brave enough to sit and ask for money—not an easy thing to do. You also need a tape recorder with a tape of the voices. We recommend that you use a variety of different sounding voices. A good brainstorming session for ideas helps.

It's also a good idea to have watchers—people who watch over the action and ensure the actor's safety. This is a good tip for any action that you do: always have someone nearby, and a little outside the action, who can deal with any problems that arise—from police, rude people, or simply the common zaniness of life.

ACTION 12

Fishing in the Sewers

FUN 🦋🦋½   RISK ½   RESOURCES 🖐

I TRIED THIS ACTION on a city street in Calgary. Two people sit on lawn chairs on the edge of the sidewalk, on either side of a sewer. They are holding fishing poles, apparently fishing in the sewer. The two people can be dressed up—if you want—and from time to time should complain about never getting a bite.

A short distance away another person hands out handbills explaining the action, with a petition or letter ready. Or you can have a sign in front of the fisher-folk explaining what is going on.

WHY FISHING IN THE SEWERS?

This action gives voice to water issues—the freshwater shortage that the Earth is facing is one of the most serious problems on this planet. The action can also focus on our daily use of water, or on what we put down our sewers and never think about again, and it can ask passersby to consider their own water consumption. The idea of fishing in a place as polluted as our

sewer system easily connects to the issue of contamination of our food and water supply, as well as to the state of our oceans.

This action brings all of those connected concerns to the surface. Combining it with a petition for stronger water pollution controls, information on the water shortage problem, or daily consumption statistics makes this an effective action.

WHAT YOU NEED

To start, you need to do a little research on water issues and decide on a focus for the action. You can probably get all the information, and angles, you need from environmental groups in your area. Canadian scientist and environmentalist David Suzuki provides water statistics in most of his books, and information can also be gleaned from the David Suzuki Foundation ‹davidsuzuki.org› or Council of Canadians ‹councilofcanadians.org› websites—there are myriad other Internet sources, too. After collecting what you need, make up a handbill, petition, and letter or sign. Many of these materials are probably already available through the organizations you consulted for research purposes.

Other than that, all you need to perform your action are two people who like to complain plus two fishing rods, two lawn chairs, and a sewer in a busy spot of town.

Gas Mask Car–Shopping

ACTION 13

FUN 🦋🦋🦋🦋 | RISK ⚠️⚠️ | RESOURCES 👤👤

THIS IS ONE OF THE funniest actions on two wheels. Before taking to the streets of Quebec City in April 2001 to demonstrate for a new world and against the FTAA, a group I was involved with called FUNK (Fighting Unaccountable Naughty Korporations) went to the local army surplus store to purchase gas masks. Later on we wanted to do something fun with the new toys, and that's where gas mask car-shopping originated.

Two people wearing gas masks walk into a car dealership to look at cars. They wander around the sales floor, mingling with customers, ready to talk and ask questions and armed with statistics regarding car pollution that they can throw out to the other customers.

In our experience, when we did this the looks from both the customers and the sales staff were priceless. We continued to walk around, appearing to be interested in various makes and models, chatting with each other about torque and power trains and using other car-related jargon. It only took the salespeople a few minutes to get over their confusion and approach us—amazingly, despite our appearance, they still seemed to think that we might just be willing buyers. That is when our questions began. How does the fuel efficiency of this vehicle compare to a bicycle? How much pollution does a car release compared to a person walking? What effect will this car have on greenhouse gas emissions? The sales persons tried their best to answer, but for the most part were left shaking their heads as we left the store and proceeded to the next dealership.

WHY GAS MASK CAR-SHOPPING?

First, this action is fun if you don't mind getting hassled by, or alienating yourself from, people who work and shop in car dealerships. Second, it

brings two realities face to face. Consumer magazines are always expounding on the fuel efficiency of this car compared to that car, but they seldom if ever stop to compare a car to a bicycle. This action throws the bicycle and other modes of transportation into the picture. At the very least, it brings some facts about car pollution to light, and it just might influence some shoppers' decisions. Just knowing that an SUV is less fuel-efficient than a Model T Ford should worry us all.

WHAT YOU NEED

Good statistics on car pollution are a start. Next, you need two gas masks. Painters' masks will do, but gas masks have a better look. Then you need two people ready and willing to bring forth the issues and possibly get kicked out of the store.

If you invite media to this action, your timing becomes important, because you want the reporters to catch the action in full swing. If you decide to do a media release, you need to discuss with your group beforehand what you want to say to the journalists. Using handbills is also a great way of clarifying your message.

An Action a Day

ACTION 14 *Radioactive Garbage–Picking*

FUN ❄❄❄½ RISK △ RESOURCES 👤👤½

THIS ACTION IS similar to *Gas Mask Car-Shopping* (Action 13). This time, however, you and your group dress up in radiation suits, the closer to the real ones the better. Then all you need to do is walk down the street picking up garbage and acting as if everything you find is hazardous material. You have a sign on the back of your suit, or you carry a sign and handbills, to explain the purpose of your action. For example, "Please help clean up the Earth before disaster strikes."

Your action can be completely silent, or you can talk and interact with each other and the crowd.

WHY RADIOACTIVE GARBAGE-PICKING?

Like gas mask car-shopping, radioactive garbage-picking presents an image of a reality that may not be far off. It is dramatic enough to grab a lot of attention, and people will be interested in what you are doing. Displaying one main message on your backs or on signs or handbills tells your audience what's going on. But you can also let folks figure it all out for themselves. You can choose to address the personal polluting problem, encourage people to take action against corporate polluting, or both.

It's best to do this action on a busy Saturday, and it helps if it's a cool day weather-wise, because radiation suits tend to get a little warm.

WHAT YOU NEED

You need radiation suits or something close to them (white overalls with masks and rubber gloves work too). You also need a simple message, and a plan for how you are going to deal with your audience and the media. (Do you talk to them? Will you talk in gibberish? Will you have one spokesperson or many?) After laying this groundwork, you simply need the people—the more the merrier—and a location.

ACTION 15 *Corporate Aid Concert*

FUN 🦎🦎🦎🦎 | RISK ⚠ | RESOURCES 🎸🎸🎸🎸

EVERY YEAR CORPORATIONS are sued because of their environmental practices and, poor souls, lose money as a result. This action represents a chance for you to give back to those companies that experience such grief.

In Edmonton we did this action—which entails organizing a benefit concert—after the phone company, Telus, decided to raise its rates for local pay-phone calls from twenty-five to thirty-five cents. Although the extra ten cents might not seem like much to some people, for others living on low incomes (and especially those who don't have a phone at home), the increase made life considerably harder.

Since the phone company seemed to desperately need extra money (after all, it had raised its rates), we decided to organize a Telus-Aid Concert for it. We charged admission and made it clear that all proceeds were going to the big boys who never seem to have enough. In the end we raised a little money and presented it to the company, which, not surprisingly, refused to take it. So instead we donated the funds to an inner-city organization.

WHY CORPORATE AID CONCERT?

Like most of the actions in this book, this one is big on parody. By announcing that you are giving to corporations, you find another way of highlighting their environmental, human, and labour rights abuses as well as their all-consuming need for the dollar, especially the public's dollar.

This action is also a good way of getting people to rally together for a common cause in a positive and fun manner. Artists and musicians can be brought together for the event. Even the ability to galvanize members of the arts community around a political issue is enough to make this action worthwhile.

The follow-up to the concert is important, too. You should go to the headquarters of the corporation or business in question and present them with their charitable donation. It might also be fun to take them the paperwork necessary for applying for charitable status—this can be found on the appropriate government website.

WHAT YOU NEED

This action requires more preparation than the others because it takes a while to line up bands, secure a venue, get equipment, and publicize the event. If this event is going to be successful, you need to try to get as many different community groups together as possible. This extends your reach and your organizational ability. Different community groups also add to the feel of the event. A diversity of performers, theatre artists, musicians, and painters can also help you to create the fun and festive atmosphere needed to ensure success.

Next you need a place and the equipment to allow the performers to put on a good show. Community halls are great venues. Some community halls come with sound equipment, but if they don't, try local unions to see if they will donate to your cause.

Now that you have a venue, performers, and equipment, you have come to the most important part—publicity. It is important to get the word out as much as you can. Put up posters, tell everyone you know, and send out press releases.

Giant Cheques

ACTION 16

FUN ❋❋❋½ | RISK ⚠ | RESOURCES 👤👤

THIS ACTION—presenting a giant cheque to a worthy recipient—makes a great complement to a corporate aid concert (Action 15). But it can also be done all on its own. Basically all you need to do, for instance, is walk into the headquarters of the company you are doing your action against and present them with a cheque for one hour of labour for one of their workers in the Third World country where their goods are manufactured.

We first did this action for the Gap Inc. Because the Gap had no corporate headquarters in our city, we chose the biggest Gap store. Although that is not the ideal location, most stores have a policy that anything unusual must be reported to head office, so your action will eventually make its way to the intended target.

For the Gap, we had a local printer make up a giant cheque for $0.11 (eleven cents). That amount is what the Gap pays its Chinese migrant workers in Russia for sewing clothes. (More information on the Gap can be found at ‹www.globalexchange.org›.) We walked into the Gap store with the cheque, and a member of our group made a short speech to reporters and Gap customers outlining Gap's sweatshop practices. We also gave out handbills outlining the issues and suggesting ways people could take action. The action went smoothly and the manager took the cheque, which was never cashed.

We have also done this action for politicians. For example, if you are an anti-poverty activist, you might want to challenge your Minister of Social Services to live off an amount equivalent to one month of social assistance. If you are a student activist, you might want to challenge your Minister of Education or your university administrators to live off one month of the student buying allowance on your student loan.

The realm of presenting big things to powerful people is endless, really. You can also issue big invoices—this one is actually cheaper, because you don't need to go through the bank, which you have to do to get a certified cheque. All you need is a big piece of poster board. You can issue an invoice for the government in question to pay its debts to the environment, or for a corporation to pay its environmental fines.

Further down the parody line, you can also make up a big certificate of achievement in corporate or political malfeasance, or a big notice of eviction if you are, say, occupying a municipally owned house or space that has gone unused and you want to make a point about evicting the absentee owner, the city.

WHY GIANT CHEQUES?

If you want the media to show up to your event or action, you need a good visual. Giant cheques, invoices, and notices are all great ways for you to get your picture in the paper and bring light to the issue you are working on, and giving or demanding money can generally—in some way—be tied to pretty much any issue. This action is also fairly low-cost, and can be done by anyone from citizens' groups to opposition political parties to labour unions. Giant cheques get the point across, allow for the ten-second sound bite, and are non-confrontational enough to suit those who are less disposed to getting hauled out of public places or otherwise taunted by passersby.

WHAT YOU NEED

You need a giant cheque, giant invoice, or whatever giant thing you are presenting. If you want an actual certified cheque, it takes about three days to order one through the bank, and you will have to have the money in an account. A larger sum may present a problem—you could talk to people with money, like labour unions or some larger organiza- tion, and ask them to have the cheque issued.

On the upside, the likelihood of the cheque actually being cashed is quite slim. Indeed, if the recipient of the cheque *does* cash it, that is worth a press release in itself.

Once you have the cheque, come up with a short sound bite when you present it. It is very important, even if you don't get to present it to the CEO, which is likely to be the case, that you put on a good show. Go through your entire spiel in true dramatic flare. You may want to rehearse beforehand just to make sure everything goes well.

Watching TV?

ACTION 17

FUN ❄❄❄ | RiSK ½ | RESOURCES 🏃🏃🏃

I GOT THE IDEA for this action after watching one of my little cousins during a small family reunion. As people spilled food, played cards, and crossed the room to talk to one another, my cousin watched the tube for eight hours straight.

From that event I came up with the following action. Get a chair (a La-Z-Boy recliner makes a nice effect) and a television set. Set them up in the middle of a busy sidewalk, and then sit there pretending to watch the tube. People will pass you on all sides, but all you do is watch, seemingly unconscious of the outside world. On the back of your TV you can write "Kill your television," "Turn off your TV and turn on your life," or some other slogan to make your action explicit.

WHY WATCHING TV?

It seems that in many homes TV has become a member of the family. Instead of conversing, playing, or planning the revolution with one another, families spend their time transfixed by images of a reality that doesn't exist. TV has become a combination babysitter, relaxation tool, and favourite pastime. It bombards us with messages of what to buy, how to look, how to act, and how to be passive in the face of a medium that is wholly run on advertising revenues. Watching TV in the middle of the sidewalk brings a real-life scenario into an unreal setting, allowing the absurdity of TV addiction to come to the surface.

WHAT YOU NEED

A comfy chair, a television set, a remote (unless you want to get up and change the channels, but who does that any more?) and a person to sit in the chair. All the person needs to do is pretend to watch TV and block

out the rest of the world. A sign is optional. Again, it's a good idea to have one or two watchers to ensure the television watcher's safety. Good luck and good watching.

ACTION 18

Alarm Clock Wake-Up

FUN 🦨🦨🦨 | RISK ⚠️⚠️⚠️½ | RESOURCES 👆👆👆½

THIS ACTION COMES from one of the masters of mayhem—Abbie Hoffman. Done with a small group of people, it can be carried out anywhere, but schools, offices, or shopping malls are the easiest targets—and for students in a class in university, this action is perfect.

Each member of the group takes an alarm clock or some other clock that rings to the chosen venue. The members spread out and sit here and there around the place, and they set their clocks to go off at various times. Eventually there will be an onslaught of sound and confusion. The people outside the action will not have a real sense of what is going on, but they will all know and recognize the sound of an alarm clock.

When your alarm goes off you might, for instance, pretend that the clock is reminding you to do something, and then you very dramatically go about doing it. Or you can let the clock ring and wait as the other alarms join in, or you can shut your alarm off after a while—the choice is yours.

If you perform this action in a university, be aware of your university's regulations regarding disruption of class time. Many universities have some type of code of student conduct prohibiting disruptions, which means that your action could result in negative consequences. To avoid unnecessary trouble it might be best to choose a cafeteria over a classroom as a location.

Alternative action: cellphone wake-up. You can use cellphones for this action as well. You just need someone to place calls to the cellphones of everyone in the group.

WHY ALARM CLOCK WAKE-UP?

As a society, we are dominated by the clock. At school, bells tell us when to move and when to learn. We look at our watches to tell us where we should be and how long we have to get there. We wake up to the buzzing of clocks, and we plan our days around the constant ticking. This action tries to disrupt that flow of timeboundedness by making it painfully explicit, and by setting off a wave of alarms we expose the absurdity of time-slavery. We also create a disturbance in the functioning of a system based on time.

Time is not real—it is a social construct that is relative. That is, it is relative and fluid save in a capitalist society, where all human actions must be monitored to keep production and consumption continuing apace.

WHAT YOU NEED

You need a bunch of clocks set to ring at various times. Setting them to go off just a few minutes apart works well. You also need a number of people—as many as possible—to work the alarms and spread them out—although you can do this action alone by just hiding the clocks here and there in the location and letting them go off by themselves.

After you set your clocks, sit back and watch out for the craziness to ensue. People hate the sound of bells, yet are controlled by them.

Time for a Funeral

FUN 🐾🐾🐾🐾   RISK ½   RESOURCES 👆👆👆½

THIS ACTION, AS old as the hills, can be used to highlight pretty much any of the decisions made by governments these days, when public policy seems to revolve around cutting back on, or privatizing, public education, health care, and anything else that fills a widespread need or exhibits a social conscience.

In post-secondary education, right across the country, tuition has been increasing at unparalleled levels. Due to government underfunding, universities in province after province are moving to differential rates, which means they can increase a single faculty's tuition above and beyond general increases. Deregulation is allowing universities to set their own tuition levels based on market models. This has brought tuition increases as high as 410 per cent in a single year. Education is quickly becoming inaccessible for students from low- or middle-income backgrounds. In 2003 the University of Alberta sought not only to increase general tuition levels by 6.3 per cent, but also to introduce differential rates for law, medicine, and business, almost doubling those faculties' tuition levels in just two years.

Students at the university, seeing the change as heralding the death of accessible education in Alberta, decided to hold a funeral in its honour. A group of them built an eight-by-four-foot coffin in a garage at three o'clock in the morning. Eulogies were written, pallbearers were found, and songs were written to suit the occasion. Even a chaplain decided to come.

It was a small ceremony. The pallbearers carried the coffin to the front of the administration building. Other participants carried burning candles and sang "Amazing Grace." Programs were handed out. When the coffin was set down the chaplain opened the ceremony with a short reading. Tuition-related songs were mournfully sung, and the eulogies were given. At the end, when dust was sprinkled over the coffin, some students dramatically broke down and cried. A tombstone was presented to a member of the university's administration. The entire event lasted only forty minutes but will be long remembered.

During a time when the government is going privatization-crazy, funerals become an appropriate response to the madness.

WHY TIME FOR A FUNERAL?

This action works because it delivers a clear and resounding message, and it is difficult for anyone—and especially the press—to take it out of context.

A mock funeral also offers an abundance of different roles for participants, so it's inclusive and allows everyone to use their talents. Activists can hum, sing, make a coffin, give a speech, organize volunteers, or carry a candle.

A funeral is one of the most symbolic actions in our society. When you do this action, you are using that symbolism—religious and otherwise—so it is important to show respect for the ceremony.

When the government seeks to cut funding or privatize a service, emotions can run high. A funeral action allows people to release their emotions in a positive way.

WHAT YOU NEED

This action can be done with varying degrees of preparation, depending on time and resources. If you don't have much time, a few candles and some grim-looking people singing sad songs can put on a pretty good show. If you have the time, you can add to the action by introducing a coffin and some crosses, and enlisting the help of friendly clergy.

You can make up your own little program outlining the day's events and explaining the issues—you can download format for these programs off the Internet. The program becomes a kind of fact sheet for the press and other onlookers, and also adds to the visual component of the action. It's also fun to get people in the community—especially those who are being harmed by the government policy in question—to do eulogies, and you can then give the press the opportunity to interview them.

Die-In or Sleep-In

FUN 💥💥💥💥 RISK ⚠️⚠️ to ⚠️⚠️⚠️½ RESOURCES 👆👆👆½
depending on location

THIS ACTION IS ESPECIALLY effective if you have a large number of people, or at least more than twenty. I first saw it carried out at a World Petroleum Conference, held in Calgary in 1999. The action took place in front of the corporate headquarters of Canada's largest oil company, Talisman Energy, a company with a history of involvement in the Sudan. At the time Talisman had been implicated in funding the Sudanese government's war against the country's own people in the largely Christian region in the south.

As the march against the WPC wound its way through the streets of Calgary, it stopped at Talisman's office building. A small affinity group* that was leading the action put the word out to the crowd that all we would need to do at a certain point was scream and then lie down on the ground and stay there. To begin, though, the affinity group performed a short play dramatizing Talisman's human rights and environmental abuses. A few actors represented the oil giant, and a larger group took on the part of the people of Sudan. Eventually the "oil reps" took out jerry cans labelled "oil"—filled with tomato juice to represent blood. They doused the "people of Sudan" in oil. The victims began to scream, were joined in that screaming by the crowd, and soon a sea of people fell to the ground, motionless. The effect was breathtaking—for minutes no one moved, all the people on the ground just stayed there, motionless. After a while, led by members of the affinity group, everyone got up, the "blood" was cleaned up, and the march continued.

For sleep-ins, the action is the same and the messaging is simple. Placards or signs saying "This _____ is making me tired" are

---

* An affinity group is basically a group of people who go into action together. It is made up of a small number of people—anywhere from about five to twenty—who form a self-sufficient support system to work on direct action or other projects. As an ACT UP Civil Disobedience website puts it: "Feelings of being isolated or alienated from the movement, the crowd, or the world in general can be alleviated through the familiarity and trust which develops when an affinity group works and acts together." ‹www.actupny.org/documents/CDdocuments/Affinity›

enough to let everyone know what you're doing and why. Sleeping bags and pillows are nice props for this one, but depending on your location you should be prepared to have them confiscated if the police grow tired of you.

WHY DIE-IN OR SLEEP-IN?

Sleep-ins or die-ins deliver clear and effective messages. Watching a large crowd of people scream to the heavens and then collapse to the ground, lifeless, is an amazing experience. The visuals are fantastic and make the action.

This action also takes up space. This is one of the fringe benefits, because you basically become a human barricade blockading any entrance or area you want to occupy. The action is a great way of starting a sit-in (occupation) or blockade (see Actions 51, 52). The act of sitting conveys only sitting, but being "tired" or "dead" communicates something more and shines a new light on the issue you are engaged with.

The theatrical nature of a die-in or sleep-in guarantees that there will be public interest. This is sometimes the biggest reward, because the people walking by and taking note of the event will be better informed about your issue. If you give out handbills, onlookers may even take action—or, better yet, join your group or organization.

WHAT YOU NEED

This action doesn't require much more than bodies. After you have the people, find a location and sleep/die away. A couple of banners and some explanatory material are the only other suggested props—other than cans of tomato juice, depending on the issue you are confronting. If appropriate, the "blood" adds to the visual effect and can be that extra punch you need to get the message across. Remember, though, if you use that kind of substance as an added effect, you should also bring along something to clean it up afterwards. If what you use stains the area, you can be charged with destruction of property.

Billboard Liberation

ACTION 21

FUN ❋❋❋½ | RISK ⚠⚠⚠⚠⚠ | RESOURCES ☂☂☂☂

BILLBOARD LIBERATION is yet another long-standing art. Ever since bill-boards became an advertising mainstay—littering our visual space—there have also been activists willing to liberate them.

There are three main tactics in billboard liberating: felling, trashing, and reclaiming.

Felling: is where you take down the entire structure of a billboard—an action that, for obvious reasons, is best carried out on a secluded rooftop or in the country. Wood is much easier to fell than metal. IMPORTANT: Do not try to fell a billboard without first reading the book *EcoDefense: A Field Guide to Monkeywrenching*.* Felling is an art and requires practice.

Reclamation: is the most effective method of billboard liberation after felling, which is much higher risk. All your group needs is spray paint and a catchy slogan. For instance:

> ORIGINAL: Molson ad—"He gets the beer, she gets the vase."
> RECLAIMED: "He gets the beer, she get the sexist asshole."

> ORIGINAL: Skinny woman selling something.
> RECLAIMED: Skinny woman with "feed me" on her chest.

Trashing: involves making a billboard completely unreadable. Balloons or light bulbs filled with paint are easy to acquire, can be launched from a distance, and get the job done. The downside is that trashing can be quite messy, so wear clothes you can dispose of quickly and easily. Trashing isn't as effective as reclamation, but is great for those hard-to-reach billboards, or if you have a paintball gun and want to have some fun.

---

* by Dave Foreman and Bill Heywood, 3rd ed. (Chico, Cal.: Abbzug Press, 1993).

An Action a Day

WHY BILLBOARD LIBERATION?

Instead of answering this question myself, I will defer to the experts at the Billboard Liberation Front ("marketing for the people") <www.billboardliberation.com>.

> In the beginning was the Ad. The Ad was brought to the consumer by the Advertiser. Desire, self worth, self image, ambition, hope; all find their genesis in the Ad. Through the Ad and the intent of the Advertiser we form our ideas and learn the myths that make us into what we are as a people. That this method of self definition displaced the earlier methods is beyond debate. It is now clear that the Ad holds the most esteemed position in our cosmology.

> ✸ Advertising suffuses all corners of our waking lives; it so permeates our consciousness that even our dreams are often indistinguishable from a rapid succession of TV commercials.

> ✸ Different forms of media serve the Ad as primary conduits to the people. Entirely new media have been invented solely to streamline the process of bringing the Ad to the people.

> ✸ You can switch off/smash/shoot/hack or in other ways avoid Television, Computers and Radio. You are not compelled to buy magazines or subscribe to newspapers. You can sic your Rottweiler on door-to-door salesmen. Of all the types of media used to disseminate the Ad there is only one that is entirely inescapable to all but the bedridden shut-in or the Thoreauian misanthrope. We speak, of course, of the Billboard. . . .

> ✸ For these reasons the Billboard Liberation Front states emphatically and for all time herein that to Advertise is to Exist. To Exist is to Advertise. Our ultimate goal is nothing short of a personal and singular Billboard for each citizen. Until that glorious day for global communications when every man, woman and child can scream at or sing to the world in 100Pt. type from their very own rooftop; until that day we will continue to do all in our power to encourage the masses to use any means possible to commandeer the existing media and to alter it to their own design.

WHAT YOU NEED

Note: Consult the *EcoDefense* guide for details on felling or destruction.

In reclamation projects, it is best to go to the site in teams of four or five, with at least two watchers, one sprayer, and one spotter. The spotter ensures the safety of the sprayer, looks for anyone who can see the sprayer, and warns the sprayer of possible dangers. The watchers should both have some form of communication device—walkie-talkies are cheap and effective. The watchers should be stationed in an area that has good sightlines and offers as much lead time as possible for the sprayer.

Dark clothes are preferable for nighttime adventures. If you are daring daytime raiders, the best attire is construction-style outfits—the ones with the flashy vests. Everyone—especially the sprayer—should wear gloves and clothes that they can discard after the action.

This is one action in which having a car can really come in handy, but if you are reclaiming billboards in busy urban areas, you may well be better off using bikes for your getaway. A white van with a ladder is best for daytime artists.

Other than that, you need spray paint, a good nozzle, and running shoes.

Stop Sign Reclamation

ACTION 22

FUN ✺✺✺½ | RISK ⚠⚠⚠⚠ | RESOURCES ✊✊½

THIS ACTION IS MUCH less risky than billboard reclamation, but can be just as effective.

I saw a stop sign reclamation on a city street just after President Bush Jr. invaded Iraq in the spring of 2003. On the bottom of a stop sign

someone had pasted a red and white sticker with the words "George W. Bush"—so the message as a whole nicely read "STOP George W. Bush."

This is an easy, inexpensive action, with the added bonus that there are stop signs absolutely everywhere.

WHY STOP SIGN RECLAMATION?

The greatest strengths of stop sign liberation are its ease and low risk, and that anyone can do it. You can plaster your message all over the place. The simplicity of the messaging also makes it accessible to the public: STOP wearing fur, STOP clear-cutting, STOP sexism—the sky is the limit on this one.

WHAT YOU NEED

Not much. You can use sticker paper with a message written or printed on it, or ordinary paper with wheat paste (flour and water) to make it stick. I prefer to go with sticker paper, even though it might cost more. Red sticker paper and black writing is best, because it blends in with the sign and creates the most aesthetically pleasing image. Sticker paper is also easier to apply—sometimes using wheat paste can result in an unsightly mess. Sticker paper is also easier to carry around with you, which makes for an easy getaway.

ACTION 23

Out of Order

FUN 🎇🎇🎇½   RISK ⚠⚠⚠⚠   RESOURCES 👆👆½

MANY UNIVERSITY campuses have monopoly deals with Coke or Pepsi. While you can't do much about your campus having been sold out to the sugar-water behemoths, you can mess with their profits. Use self-adhesive sticker labels and a word-processing program to create sheets of "OUT OF ORDER" stickers. Then go around campus putting them over the coin slots of the vending machines. It will be a while before anyone figures out that the labels aren't for real, and in the meantime you have messed with the profits of a monopolistic corporation.

WHY OUT OF ORDER?

Many of these monopoly deals were introduced in the mid-1990s with little or no public debate. On some campuses there has been little resistance to so-called "single source beverage deals," even though these deals provide far more benefits to the corporations than they do to the students. Furthermore, cash-strapped public schools are having to cut deals with soda-pop multinationals just to buy textbooks and materials.

This action makes it clear that resistance to this agenda does exist, and it offers you an easy and inexpensive way of expressing that resistance.

WHAT YOU NEED

Sticker paper, someone who knows how to make labels, and a computer and printer. Two people are best for the actual action of slapping on the stickers—one to act as a cover and the other to do the sticking. Make sure there are no security cameras around, and off you go.

ACTION 24

Tent-In

FUN 🐝🐝🐝 to 🐝🐝🐝🐝 ½ | RISK ⚠️⚠️ ½ | RESOURCES 👤👤👤 ½
depending on weather

THIS IS AN EASY one for the outdoor enthusiast. A group of us did it in minus-thirty-five- degree weather on the lawn of University Hall, the university's main administrative building, to protest tuition increases. Our messages were "We Will Freeze for the Fees" and "Tenting against Tuition." The action started with only six people, two of whom were paid university staff. We set up our tents, had piles and piles of blankets, and pretty much froze together all night.

The following day we set up a more prolonged presence. We got a bunch of tarps and created a large shelter, dragged a picnic table inside, and made a few large banners to let everyone know what we were doing and why. By the end of the day we had doubled our numbers. We did a few outside activities to draw people in and start building a sense of community. We sang songs and generally had quite a good, although cold, time. Journalists would sporadically pop by to see what we were up to.

By the fifth day of the campaign we had a tent city. Over seventy-five people were camping out; the tents covered the entire lawn. People were bringing us hot chocolate and coffee. Most of the campus knew why we were there, and for the most part supported our efforts. People came by to chat or wish us good luck. By the end of the week we had made the national news and brought news of the crisis facing post-secondary education to thousands of households across Canada.

In a prolonged campaign, tent-ins allow you to pick up momentum and people as you go along. The longer the campaign—if you can maintain it and keep growing—the better the visuals.

WHY TENT-IN?

This is a good type of action to do when you believe that an issue has the ability to grow, to create a sustained presence, and you really want to put some heat on the decision- makers. Tent-ins take up space and have great media appeal because the press can have complete access to the tent city. The media also love anything that smacks of civil disobedience. Anything that bleeds or is illegal will usually make the news. A tent-in may or may not be illegal, depending on where you set it up, but regardless of the legal circumstances, tent-ins *appear* to be illegal. The media will therefore be all over the action.

Tent-ins also force people to pay attention to you. In our case, as we were camped outside University Hall, all of the administrators had to pass us every time they went in or out of the building. They couldn't cover us up or push us into a private meeting room. As an added bonus, all the business leaders coming to the university for meetings were made aware of the action and the issues. It was impossible to ignore us.

WHAT YOU NEED

The basics are people and tents, but for this action to be really successful you need two other key elements: a community of supporters or concerned people and some great visuals. A community atmosphere is essential if you want your tent city to grow. People in your tent city need to feel welcome, and you should have a good time while you are there. This means that you need to come up with activities. You should have hot chocolate, musical instruments, playing cards, board games, portable radios, ghetto blasters—anything that will help you build and maintain a positive atmosphere. The worst thing that can happen is that spirits start to fade and the people participating grow cranky and tired.

The community also has to be welcoming to others. Be friendly to anyone who stops. Tell them they are welcome to join you. If people do bring their tents, help them set the tents up. The more things you can do to create a positive community, the better. If you have the resources to feed people, that feature alone can do wonders. Local unions often have supplies on hand of pancake mix or other food, and cooking grills. Ask them to donate, and they probably will.

You should have a banner that says who you are and what you are doing, and that encourages others to join in. If the news media take even one picture of your banner or interview you in front of it, you get your message out to the wider world. The more signs you have around the camp, the better. You want to make sure that if and when the media show up, regardless of what they shoot or write, you will get your message out—and the signs will help you do that.

ACTION 25 — *T-Shirt-Making (Ask Me about East Timor)*

FUN 🐝🐝🐝 | RISK 0 | RESOURCES 🪶🪶🪶½

LOTS OF PEOPLE make T-shirts with messages emblazoned on their fronts or backs. This little number is a spin on a traditional T-shirt action that I liberated from a group in San Francisco.

If you have information you want to share with others, say so on a T-shirt. Mine says, "Ask me about East Timor." It works—I've had person after person come up to me and ask me about it. It leads to a lot of conversations and even some good friends. We now use T-shirts for every action we are working on.

WHY T-SHIRT-MAKING?

Most activists have tons of knowledge about a variety of issues. The problem is that these issues don't come up in everyday conversation.

The only time you get to talk about it is with people who already know the issues. The T-shirt opens up the possibility of dialogue with strangers, which is always a good thing. People also want to know about different issues but often don't know where to get information, and political events, teach-ins, and that sort of thing can be intimidating (or possibly even boring) for the average person. A one-on-one conversation allows you to clarify points and answer questions.

WHAT YOU NEED

You can put slogans on T-shirts or fabric in a number of different ways.

1. You can do it freestyle by using a paintbrush and acrylic paints broken down with fabric medium (either use two-thirds paint and one-third fabric medium or half-half if you want the paint to be thinner and less opaque). And of course you need an old T-shirt. After you are done painting, let the shirt dry for twenty-four hours, and for a long-lasting result simply turn the T-shirt inside out and iron it with low heat.

2. You can use a stencil. A wise womin named Coreen taught me how to use thin plastic as a stencil. This plastic can be found at any store that sells school supplies. You're looking for a thin yet rigid plastic, like the plastic used for overheads or clear portfolios. Then you can use stencils or your own creation to write a slogan and/or design on the plastic. Use a sharp knife to cut the stencil out (preferably over a cutting board). Then put the stencil over any T-shirt or fabric and start painting away (again, acrylic paint plus fabric medium).

The advantages of this method are that you can use the stencil over and over, and it can also be used on hard surfaces. You can also use spray paint for stencilling on hard surfaces.

3. Another way of doing it is to use a cheap silkscreening method. For this you need sheer curtain material, which can usually be found in second-hand stores. You also need four fairly thin lengths of wood for the outer edge of the frame (usually one inch wide by one inch thick or one by one and a half, and whatever length you want for the size of the frame), and about fifty flat tacks and grout sealer. Connect the pieces of wood together into the shape of a frame. You can either use screws or nails (screws work better). It is very important that you create a flat surface when making this frame and that none of the frame edges can twist around. Next cut out a piece of the sheer curtain material so that each side of the material goes about one inch outside each edge of the frame. Then, using the tacks, start tacking the material to the frame. The objective is to stretch the fabric so that it fits tightly over the frame.

Tip: start tacking half on one side of the frame and then half on the opposite side and so forth until the material covers the frame tightly (caution: making it too tight can rip the material).

Next, turn your frame around so that the flat screen faces the direction of the ground and write your message and/or make your design on the new screen using grout sealer. You may want to write your message out first with a pencil (not with a felt pen). Let the frame dry for twenty-four hours. Put the frame towards light and fill in the little holes found where you used the grout sealer. Wherever there are holes the paint will seep through. Let dry for another twenty-four hours and then you can start using your new silkscreening frame. Put the flat, tacked surface on any piece of fabric and paint over the screen.

The paint should only seep through where there is no grout sealer painted on the screen. Therefore, whatever you paint with the grout sealer, the opposite will show up on your fabric. If you want the letters of a message to show up in paint, you would then have to paint the grout sealer around the contours of the letters. You can use the screen a few times in a row before rinsing it out with water. Make sure the paint does not dry on the frames. Remember to use fabric medium with your acrylic paint.

4. Maybe the easiest way: you can now buy iron-on paper that will work in your computer printer; so you can take an image from a computer file or from the Internet, print it out, and then you just need to iron it on a T-shirt.

ACTION 26

Mock Protests

FUN 🦁🦁🦁 | RISK ⚠️⚠️⚠️ ½ | RESOURCES 👤👤

SOMETIMES THE BEST way of bringing attention to an issue is to take support of it to the extreme, by staging an ironic protest. Here are three examples of mock protests.

Walk for Capitalism. This is an event founded by Prodos, an Australian radio host, street singer, and right-wing activist (an admirer of Ayn Rand). The event, which occurs worldwide every year, advertises itself as being "For the love of freedom! And the glory of human creativity!— Worldwide rallies, concerts, debates, awards, street parties, workshops, fun and festivities!" In 2001 a group of us infiltrated their march dressed in business suits and carrying signs: "Profits before People," "The

Environment Is for Suckers," "Local Sucks, Buy from Multinationals." We gave media interviews on behalf of the organizing group and made the entire thing look even more absurd than it already was.

Arms Show. When an arms show came to town, we were there with signs saying "Why Wait? Destroy the World Today." We even went into the conference and set up a makeshift booth for "The Button," a device that would destroy the world. We were there for fifteen minutes before we were discovered, but our message was picked up by the press and got through to others inside the meetings.

Anti-Choice Rally. At most anti-choice events, you have the usual clashes between the two sides on the issue. This time we decided to stage a mock protest and reveal the absurdity of the anti-choice movement. With carefully placed signs—"Every Egg Is Sacred" and "Menstruation Should Be Abolished, Each Egg Should Be Fertilized"— we were able to deliver a pro-choice message in a unique way. This one is a little more dangerous, especially if you are a woman. Go with a group.

WHY MOCK PROTESTS?

In the activist community, in protest situations, people get tired of the same old messages and need a little levity. The mock protest can reveal the absurdity of your opponents' arguments. Mock protests are also a great infiltration device. Groups that you fundamentally disagree with often hold events to gain support and raise money. Doing a mock protest jams the event and can dissuade people from joining.

But use this action with caution because it can be dangerous being on the inside of a hostile crowd.

WHAT YOU NEED

Signs and messages. You need to make sure that your messages are absurd enough that people realize you are being ironic. You don't want the press to take you seriously—unless you want to do a media hoax (see Action 31).

Pie-Slinging

ACTION 27

FUN 🦖🦖🦖🦖 | RISK ⚠⚠⚠⚠ ½ | RESOURCES 👆

IF YOU CAN'T trust 'em, crust 'em. This is the rally call for the Biotic Baking Brigade, an international organization dedicated to giving corrupt politicians and CEOs their just deserts. In 1999 the group was calling for a new kind of global uprising:

> As multinational corporations accelerate the plunder of our world during these last days before the millennium, a militant resistance has formed in response. Diverse in philosophy and targets, diffuse in geography and structure, the movement comprises freedom-loving people with a sense of aplomb and gastronomics. Fighting a guerrilla media and ground war with the titans of industry, these revolutionary bakers and pie-slingers have achieved in short order what can truly be called a global pastry uprising. This uprising has its roots in the belief that our planet is not dying, it is being killed; and the ones doing the killing have names and faces.
>
> Since last October, over 40 prominent corporate executives, politicians, economists, and sell-out NGO "leaders" have received their just deserts for crimes against people and the land. The groups and individuals involved in this unique form of Pie-rect Action have declared their opposition to the neoliberal platform: clear governments out of the way; deregulate financial markets; hoodwink citizens into trusting "the invisible thumb" of the market to protect them; and legislate corporate domi-

nance through such trade agreements as NAFTA, GATT and the MAI.*

There is one large problem here: under our judicial system, actions like those of the Biotic Baking Brigade or Les Entartistes, based in Quebec, are illegal, and you can be charged if you participate in them—including assault with a weapon if the pie is hot enough. That said, the Brigade has a long history of action (see its website at **‹www.bioticbakingbrigade.org›**). For Les Entartistes, see **‹www.entartistes.ca›**.

For the jail- and fine-averse, there is a legal variation on the pieing theme that can be used as a fundraiser as well as to raise issues. We have all either been to or seen on TV pie-throwing contests in which local celebrities stick their heads out of a hole in a wall and get cream pies chucked at them for a good cause. In the action we are suggesting, since most corporate criminals do not want to appear at your events, you can make masks of corporate criminals or their political lackeys, get a courageous friend to don one, and get eager participants to line up and throw away. You can make masks by downloading pictures of the

---

* "A Treatise on the Global Pastry Uprising by Agent Apple, Biotic Baking Brigade, General Command," Ecotopia, *The Ecologist* (UK), Summer 1999.

pie targets off the Internet, laminating them if you want them to last, and taping them to a plastic mask.

This event is a great stress reliever and can actually raise some cash.

WHY PIE-SLINGING?

The treatise of the Biotic Baking Brigade pretty much speaks for itself, but it's worth repeating that more people need to have their "just deserts." Embarrassing someone in public is sometimes the best way of ensuring that a message gets heard loud and clear. A pieing will almost certainly be covered in the news, and it may even hurt the company's bottom line or blemish the politician's reputation.

The legal version of pieing can do a few things: highlight an issue of community concern (local, national, international); provide people with a fun way of releasing stress; and raise money. For instance, you can highlight the craziness of the president of the United States—whether he is advocating oil drilling in Alaska or invading a foreign country—or the machinations of the Canadian prime minister, or you can address a more local issue. Unfortunately, people are more likely to pay attention to a pie-throwing contest than they are to attend a rally. Better yet, the contest can be part of a larger rally.

WHAT YOU NEED

A large board with holes for people to stick their heads through, whipped cream, and pie plates. You also need an image to represent the political or corporate criminal. This can be a full mask from a costume store, or a photocopied and blown-up picture pasted onto a piece of cardboard.

Puppet-Making

ACTION **28**

FUN 🐏🐏🐏½ | RISK ⚠ | RESOURCES ☂☂☂☂

ANYTIME YOU CAN use a puppet, do so—this is another golden rule of actions. We try to use puppets all the time. My favourite puppet moment was when Prime Minister Jean Chrétien came to town. We heard about the prime minister's plans to give a short speech outside a local Liberal MP's office, and so we turned the same-sex kissing booth (see Action 29) into a corporate confessional booth—lining it with corporate symbols. We set it down outside the office and had an actor representing a corporate priest, and me as a giant Chrétien puppet. The puppet was only a head puppet, but once on my head turned me into a figure about eight feet tall. The puppet was impossible to ignore, especially with megaphone in hand.

Once in place, Puppet Chrétien confessed his sins to the corporate priest, but it wasn't until the real Chrétien arrived that the fun began. Puppet Chrétien introduced itself to Jean Chrétien, then tried to proceed inside the MP's office to deliver a speech. The puppet was stopped and refused entry. However, the puppet did not go quietly—instead it threatened to pepper-spray the crowd.

Eventually the real Jean Chrétien delivered his speech to the crowd gathered outside, but of course puppet Chrétien was there too. The flow of Jean Chrétien's speech was perfect, because it allowed Puppet Chrétien to respond to each line. When the prime minister said he had balanced the budget, Puppet Chrétien would list the social programs that were cut to do so. When Chrétien talked about job creation, Puppet Chrétien was right there to say that most of the jobs created were minimum-wage, which means that the workers don't even meet the poverty line. And when Chrétien thanked the organizers, puppet Chrétien thanked the corporations that had funded the Liberal campaign.

The action was so effective that it made the gathered Liberal supporters laugh—proving once again the benefit of doing actions with a sense of humour. The crowd could well have become hostile, but this good-natured, fun approach instead brought them to laughter, and even to a kind of participation in the show. Actions are always about bringing out issues, not attacking people.

WHY PUPPET-MAKING?

Puppets are fantastic. They enable you to be anything from the prime minister to a giant needle to a dragon. Through the use of puppets, you can distil complex issues into simple stories that are accessible to everyone.

A generic rally can be brought to life with puppets, or one puppet can be a stand-alone action. Puppets tend to ensure that you will get media coverage and that you'll be able to get your message out.

Making a puppet can also be a great community-building activity. It takes a couple of afternoons to fully construct a large puppet, but the results are worth it.

WHAT YOU NEED

What you need depends on the type of puppet you want to make. Puppets can be made of clay, cardboard, papier mâché, or anything under the sun. Whatever supplies you have, chances are you can make a puppet out of it. The booklet *Wise Fool Basics* is a great resource for giant puppet-making that teaches you how to make several different styles and sizes of puppets.*

A puppet like the one we made for the Jean Chrétien action can be built in ten easy steps. All you need is some corrugated cardboard, available in large rolls for about ten dollars at supply stores, as well as glue or flour and water, paper and paint. Then follow the simple directions, and remember to think about the message you want to deliver—make sure it's not just a puppet, but a puppet with your message, or slogan, on it.

Same-Sex Kissing Booth

FUN ❄❄❄❄❄   RISK ⚠   RESOURCES 👤👤

MY FIRST-EVER KISS with a boy happened at this action designed by my partner. Stockwell Day of the Canadian Alliance Party—now part of the new Conservative Party of Canada—was one of the easiest targets ever to hit the Canadian political scene. He has spoken out against abortion and gay rights, and has been accused of being racist as well. During his campaign across Canada in the 2000 federal election, Stockwell stopped in Edmonton for two nights. First Nations groups, women's organizations, members of gay, lesbian, bisexual, transgendered (GLBT) groups, and other activists all came out to a protest against him on his first night in town. The small group I was with brought three things to the protest: a giant puppet (see Action 28), the corporate whore action (Action 41), and a same sex-kissing booth.

The booth generated significant media attention and ended up being the catalyst for a great photo of me kissing a boy. The shot appeared in

---

* *Wise Fool Basics: A Handbook of Our Core Techniques*, by K. Ruby and the Art and Revolution Street Theater Collective, 5th ed. (Berkeley, Cal.: Wise Food Puppet Interventions, 2001).

The Edmonton Sun—and it eventually even garnered a prize for the photographer.

WHY SAME-SEX KISSING BOOTH?

Effective actions use cultural familiarity and symbolism to make their points. Kissing booths carry that symbolic baggage for most North Americans. The same-sex component twists the symbol and amplifies the point of your action.

This action is fun—it enables you to get a little closer to your friends and bring awareness to a persecuted community in our society. It is inclusive and allows everyone to participate, if you are willing to confront social norms. The visuals are great and the message is clear. The kissing booth doesn't require any rehearsal or lines, which is always an asset.

WHAT YOU NEED

The first thing you need is a booth—and this can be as simple as ours was at the Stockwell Day event: a refrigerator box with a sign. It could be as complicated as a wooden stand, like an old school kissing booth (see also Action 10, *Information Booth*). In this case I prefer the cardboard variety. Even though you lose a little of the visual, a cardboard booth is easy to make and easy to transport. You can strap it to the roof of a car.

After that, all you need is an appropriate location, some willing participants, and you are ready to kiss and tell.

WHENEVER MAJOR politicians come to town, they bring their own security, which makes it difficult for activists to get close enough to ask questions, engage them in a conversation (with a puppet?), or offer them a big cheque for services (not) rendered. So the trick is to bring along your own security personnel.

We did this in 2001 when the federal Liberal Party held a convention in Edmonton. The main item on the agenda was planning for the following year's G8 summit, to be held in Kananaskis, Alberta. The delegates included the prime minister. Three of us drove to the Mayfield Convention Centre in a 1980 Toyota Corolla hatchback. When we emerged from the car we were in complete security apparel: a suit, dark sunglasses, shiny shoes, and a fake earpiece. We had also brought along a safety vest, which we left in the car for the second half of the action.

Leaving one person outside, two of us walked into the centre and positioned ourselves on either side of the main door. For some reason—perhaps due to the large security presence, bad communication, simple ineptitude, or because we really played our roles well—we didn't arouse suspicion, at least at first.

We started by nodding at the delegates as they passed, periodically fingering our fake earpieces. As we began to feel comfortable we were able to stop delegates, pull them aside—we even frisked one—and give them information on the G8. After what seemed a long while we noticed a bit of a buzz going around about our legitimacy, and we knew it was only a matter of time before our cover would be blown and we would be removed. We escalated our action, asking delegates to declare any weapons of mass destruction and leave their terrorist legislation at the door. We did this only after we knew the media was watching; otherwise it could have been dangerous to our safety. As delegates passed we said, "Please proceed in, the other terrorists are already inside."

The scene lasted only a few minutes longer before we were escorted out. Before we left, we made a final statement about the so-called "anti-terrorism" legislation that had been passed in the wake of 9/11.

Once outside, we went back to the car, put on our safety vests, and proceeded onto the street to guide traffic, at first diverting vehicles around the building and then simply getting them to slow down so we could give them information. We were able to do this throughout the day and eventually gave out over a hundred pamphlets about the G8.

A variation: big brother. For your own public forums, events, and rallies, bring your own security. In Edmonton, for instance, at public debates, rallies, and events protesting legislation that would pave the way for private, for-profit health care in the province, two activists dressed up as security personnel with the words "Big Brother" printed on the backs of their jackets, and then wandered around amongst the crowd. This small action effectively pointed out an emerging security culture.

WHY BRING YOUR OWN SECURITY?

People have a strange attachment to listening to security guards or anyone with the veil of authority. Depending on the degree of your acceptance, pretending to be a security guard can allow you to gain ground on the establishment. If you are accepted by security authorities, what you can do is pretty wide open: you can stop delegates, enter the meeting, frisk people, stop vehicles.

The problem is that when you are discovered—and you *will* be discovered unless you get in and out very quickly—security personnel don't take kindly to people impersonating them, and they may treat you rudely (to say the least) if you don't have protection; and by protection, I don't mean Mace or a Taser stun gun, I mean the media. For this action you need to know where the cameras are and position yourself accordingly. Then you can get your message out when the time comes, and you will also ensure that you are not manhandled in the process.

It is also important that you leave the premises as soon as you are asked—but not before you get your message out to the media. You don't want to get charged for an offence, and if you leave as soon as you are asked, that is less likely to happen.

If you are not accepted as legitimate security guards, your focus can shift to making fun of the police state surrounding political officials. Make your actions larger than life—just making it known that the prime minister has to be protected by an army of police officers should, in itself, raise alarm bells.

All you need for this action is some moxie and a security outfit. You need to act like you belong. The more you sweat, fidget, or feel like you are out of place the greater the risk that you will be caught. We are constantly being surprised about how far a little confidence will take us. Be friendly but stern. Try to act like the security guards you see protecting the president in movies, or mimic real-life examples.

For your outfit, a suit and tie from your local thrift shop can do the trick. Don't go with a plaid or anything too strange—a nice solid black or dark blue is perfect. A big walkie-talkie can help give the illusion of legitimacy, especially if that is what the other security guards are carrying. An earpiece is a must—mostly just for the humour of it all. You can get one by buying the "undercover officer" kit at your local toy store. The kit will give you most of the gadgets you need for the operation.

You should also plan the message you want to deliver after you are discovered, and have some information ready to give to the press or any other individuals about what you are doing and why you are there. Solid, critical information is always key to a good action.

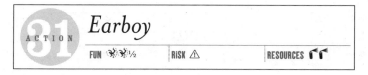

ACTION 31

Earboy

FUN 🏃🏃½   RISK ⚠   RESOURCES 👤👤

This one is not really a self-contained action, but instead more of a way of promoting a political event. We originally stumbled on this idea late one night in university residence, when we started fooling around with an announcement board and created the message "EARBOY IS COMING." We did it more as a joke than to deliver a political message and didn't think it would go anywhere.

The next day we were surprised by the reaction. Instead of people dismissing the sign as a joke, we found a group of students hanging around the information board discussing who "Earboy" was. As the day wore on the buzz grew, first over our floor and then through the entire building. All the attention caught us by surprise. We began to think, if only we had planned an event around "Earboy," we would have had quite the turnout.

WHY EARBOY?

People love a mystery. Sometimes the best way of promoting an event is not to say "come to this forum," but instead to market the event in a way that creates a mystery. By doing this you may be able to draw in people who are not normally interested in participating in such things—they just might show up out of simple curiosity.

WHAT YOU NEED

This action depends on having an initial idea, plan, or need for some kind of political event that you want to promote. Then all you need is a "mystery" idea transferred into posters and the people power to put up the posters. And of course you will have to co-ordinate the event you will hold at the end once you get people out.

Media Hoax

ACTION 32

FUN 😵😵😵   RISK ⚠️⚠️⚠️½   RESOURCES 👆👆👆👆½

A MEDIA HOAX IS basically a fictional event, product, or story that is used to highlight the flaws in media stories or to introduce a burning issue that you think is being misrepresented. Joey Skaggs is one of the best media hoax artists ever. His work has been described as "media jamming"—as action using media sabotage tactics. Often using press releases as his vehicle, he creates hoaxes that become front-page news, and in effect the press unknowingly becomes both the victim and the subject of the hoax. It's all about "media irresponsibility and the need for their audiences to question what they read," as one website article, "Master of the Hoax," puts it. The Skaggs media hoaxes outlined in the article include:

"Hair Today," a purported answer for baldness, achieved by transplanting scalps from cadavers; the "Fat Squad," a hard-line diet enforcement agency that relied on the threat of brute force to keep clients' waistlines slim; and "Dog Meat Soup," a proposal to nationwide animal shelters from a fictional Korean entrepreneur to purchase, for food consumption, dogs and cats that would otherwise be euthanized.

Skaggs also set up a hoax around the infamous O.J. Simpson trial of the early 1990s. Posing as a Dr. Bonuso, a computer scientist working in association with the New York University School of Law, Skaggs revealed a computer program named "Solomon" that applied case data input and used artificial intelligence and a virtual jury to spit out verdicts. (After a minimum of deliberation, Solomon found Simpson guilty.) The story was picked up in newspaper, TV, and radio news stories and even spilled over to legal journals. Eventually Skaggs revealed the whole thing as a hoax. To learn more about Skaggs, simply type his name into an Internet search engine—but be careful you yourself don't get hoaxed in the process.

Mastering a media hoax as well as Joey Skaggs does is a huge task. For less ambitious individuals, there are alternatives. You can do a mini-media hoax, for instance, simply by placing a classified ad in the local paper. We did this when the province deregulated electricity and bills went through the roof. People were eager to find back-up sources of energy just in case the province experienced brownouts like the one they had in California. We placed ads in *The Edmonton Journal* and *Edmonton Sun*.

Hundreds of Electrical Generators for sale
Everything Must Go!!!
Phone 427-2251 for more information

The phone number was for the Premier's Office. Over the next week, from what we were told by the classified ads editor (who had to handle the complaints), hundreds of people called inquiring about the generators. Of course, when they called the number we listed, they found out that the whole thing was a joke.

WHY MEDIA HOAX?

The news is supposed to be a place that we can turn to for a truthful representation of world and daily events. The media hoax reveals that the media do not always (if ever) know what they're doing—much less present the truth. A hoax calls the press and journalism into question—something we need to do if we want to build different, alternative kinds of media.

WHAT YOU NEED

To pull off a successful media hoax, you need imagination and a lot of planning. Some of Joey Skaggs's hoaxes lasted for over a year and required a great deal of foresight and effort. For one of his hoaxes, Skaggs had an office and a fake secretary and went into "work" every day for a year. For the "Fat Squad" dieting program, he had a team of actors all ready to raid another actor's fridge to keep him on the diet.

But it is possible to do a media hoax that involves less legwork and a shorter timeline. A small-town newspaper makes an ideal target. Small-town papers are always looking for good stories to fill the space between the ads, always in a hurry to meet their deadlines, and don't have the staff to check everything out. A well-crafted press release and some good photos are usually enough to land a story in their pages. Sometimes small-town papers will print your release virtually word for word, so draft it carefully.

Once you have an article printed in a small-town paper, you suddenly have a basis of credibility and can take your story to a paper with a larger circulation. Send out another press release, with the published article, photos, and contact information attached.

The key to this action is coming up with a strong idea—something that people will actually believe. Hot issues or subjects exploited by the media (SARS, disease-of-the-week, terrorist scares) are great places to start brainstorming. Next, it's a matter of working backwards to figure out how to make your idea successful.

Hoaxes are about manipulation, and duping people can turn them off. In this action you particularly need to think things all the way through, taking into account possible consequences and fallouts. While a lot of people dislike media hoaxes, we have to remember that the media manipulate *us* all the time, so taking that power into our own hands is only fair play.

Candlelight Vigil

FUN 🏃🏃½   RISK ½   RESOURCES 👤👤

Do not go gentle into that good night . . . rage, rage against the dying of the light.
— Dylan Thomas

CANDLELIGHT VIGILS ARE yet another of the actions that have been around for a long time, and this one might even be the oldest in the book. Candlelight vigils have been used to make statements on everything from health care to the environment, from school closings to violent deaths to war. One of the actions that stands out most in my mind is the candlelight vigil held to reflect on the slaughter of thousands of Iraqi civilians after the U.S. attacks on that country. Hundreds of gathered together, each one filing into a circle in front of the Legislature Building, each person in turn lighting a candle from the candle of the person who had come just before. Eventually we had a sea of light, hoping to cast light on an injustice a world away.

Candlelight vigils are used both to send a message to the world and to provide a place where people can mourn, reflect, and come together as a community.

WHY CANDLELIGHT VIGILS?

This action is known both for its ease and for its symbolic value. Candlelight vigils are completely inclusive—and they can take place with three people or thousands. No speeches need to be made. No chants need to be uttered, no songs sung—although you can add these features if you like.

Vigils provide people with a chance to pause and escape from the frantic pace of our society, to reflect on what is going on in the larger world. They provide a gathering point for people to come together, and especially in times of immense sorrow people have a need to be with others who are feeling the same pain.

Vigils act as a beacon. A candle has strong symbolic value in the West—as Elton John so assuredly knows. It is a symbol of hope and peace and carries meaning for most people who see it.

A variation: silent vigils. By 2004 the Sisters of Providence in Kingston, Ontario, had been keeping a weekly silent vigil in front of that Ontario city's historic City Hall for over eight years. Having started the vigils in 1995 to protest the provincial government's attack on the poor, the nuns and their supporters came to express their concerns in a little Why-Do-We-Stand-Here handout: "We stand in silent, non-violent solidarity with those affected by governments and corporations that put profits before humankind and indeed before all creation."

WHAT YOU NEED

Candlelight vigils are quite easy to organize. All you need are candles, a suitable location, and an issue that is appropriate to this type of action. You don't need a lot of people—a small group will do, though as in most actions, the more the better. You do need to check on fire regulations, depending on your location. Usually all that is required is some sort of container placed around the candle. To ensure that your message gets out, you might want to display a banner or put up a large sign. You might also have a microphone and a small amplifier hooked up (or maybe even just a bullhorn) for anyone who wants to speak to the issue.

ACTION 34

Plant-in/Guerrilla Gardening

FUN ✖✖✖½   RISK △△△   RESOURCES 🖐🖐🖐½

THIS IDEA CAME from a mass action by indigenous groups in Indonesia. While the government was building golf courses, taking up large tracts of arable land, the people were starving. So the people of Indonesia decided that if the government wasn't going to listen to them, they were going to take control of the situation and the golf courses with a massive plant-in. They planted trees, subsistence crops, threw seeds on greens and fairways, and reclaimed land that was sorely needed for survival.

Plant-ins and guerrilla gardening can also be successful in urban situations where people want more green space or where unnatural species are being planted instead of native species—or simply to highlight the issue of land being used for cars and golf courses while people continue to starve and live on the streets.

WHY PLANT-IN/GUERRILLA GARDENING?

You do a plant-in to reclaim public space, to create more green space, and to deliver a pointed message. From a security point of view this action is great, because the police find it difficult to arrest someone for planting a tree or a strawberry plant. The action also garners sympathy from onlookers. After all, most people have a special connection to plants and living things. We get a rush from seeing a beautiful tree, and many of us get all excited about the thought of planting a garden. Passersby who see your guerrilla gardening efforts being smashed by a police officer, or see you getting arrested for trying to plant a seed, tend to have a very deep and immediate reaction. Your message is received, and your action is a success.

WHAT YOU NEED

All you need is an appropriate location. It could be a property development that just went through despite public opposition, a green space that was just paved over, or (if you are particularly daring) a private golf course. If you want to communicate a general message about green space, you can plant seeds or grown flowers in the cracks of sidewalks, on the sides of streets, or in industrial wastelands that otherwise consist of nothing but dirt, scrubby grass, and concrete, day in, day out.

After you select your location, you need planting tools (a shovel is always handy), plants, and friends to help you out. Delivering your message via banners is always good, and a source of water is essential if you want your seeds or plants to thrive.

If you are true guerrillas, you can do the action at night so that anyone who comes by in the morning will get a big surprise. A group of guerrilla planters did this successfully at the University of Calgary, after the administration turned down a proposal for an organic garden on campus. Students simply took matters into their own hands and planted one anyway—the garden stands to this day. Nighttime actions require walkie-talkies, flashlights, and a bit more planning than usual.

Guerrilla gardening doesn't have to be a group action. Wildflower seeds are super cheap, grow in pretty much any climate, and, depending on the type of seed, can be scattered or planted with very little effort. Guerrilla gardening is good for your soul and is a quick and easy way to make you feel like you stuck it to the authorities in a nice way.

War of the Corporations Radio Play

ACTION 35

FUN 🐾🐾 | RISK 0 | RESOURCES 👍👍👍👍

THIS ACTION IS BASED on the famous radio broadcast that shook the world. In 1938, when people in the United States heard Orson Welles's radio play *War of the Worlds*,* they thought the world was about to end. In the drama, aliens had invaded the Earth and were destroying life on the planet. Today, while aliens have still not invaded, there is an entity that has done so, and that has not only seemingly taken over much of the world but has also brought us to the edge of an ecological precipice: the corporation. Welles's imagined drama is coming true, although only a minority of the planet's people seem to be concerned about it.

This action is more time-consuming than the others. The upside is that once someone does it, it is only a download away from being heard by people all over the world.

---

* The program is available on vintage radio program CDs or tapes, available in many libraries. It's worth a listen.

What you need first of all is permission to do an hour-long broadcast of a *War of the Corporations* radio play. Alternative, co-op, or campus stations may be willing to take a chance on airing your work. The next thing to do is transform the *War of the Worlds* drama into an updated *War of the Corporations*. The plot line of the original play is easy to transfer into a new form, and you will be surprised at how many similarities there are between the action of *War of the Worlds* and what the multinational corporations are doing to the planet.

WHY WAR OF THE CORPORATIONS RADIO PLAY?

Most community organizing manuals tell you that the golden rule is to speak to the community through community experience—things people can identify with readily and easily. With *War of the Corporations* you are using something that people are familiar with. Most people have heard about the Welles broadcast, and many people have even heard bits of it performed—or are at least familiar with the genre. Adapting the original play slightly allows you to use the already familiar cultural language for different ends.

WHAT YOU NEED

Time and people to help. A good adaptation isn't an easy thing to achieve, and it will take time, several rewrites, and patience. Then you need a friendly radio station, a cast to read all of the different parts, and for maximum coolness someone with a knowledge of sound effects. Again, people who work or volunteer at your campus radio station may be able to help you. The finished product will be worth all of your time and effort, but this one really is an undertaking. After all, no one ever said activism is easy.

Wrestling Match

FUN 🤼🤼🤼🤼 | RISK ⚠️⚠️ | RESOURCES 👆👆👆½

ARE YOU READY TO RUMBLE?In this corner we have corporate greed. In the other corner we have the people. The WWE (now it's World Wrestling Entertainment; formerly it was the WWF) is one of the most successful spectacles of our times. Regardless of the blatant sexism, racism, and general bigotry involved in this spectacle, every day millions of people watch it.

As activists we have to learn from the successes of capitalism and where appropriate use this cultural knowledge for subversive purposes. With this action, you take the well-worn script and ritual of wrestling and use it to highlight an important issue, creating an effective piece of agit-prop.

Agitprop (agitational propaganda) has a long history, dating back to its first use as the name of a Soviet Union agency for the dissemination of Communist political propaganda. But later it became known as the vehicle for delivering any direct, overtly political message. It doesn't even have to be political, it seems. Nowadays, as one source puts it, "even a television cartoon might be described as 'agitprop' if it could be interpreted as a marketing ploy to sell toys."* The term is used for any form of mass media that subtly (or not so subtly) tries to influence public opinion.

Agitprop uses stock characters, good and evil, and simple messages to deliver a strong message. Through wrestling, you already have the building blocks for the action. In this case, the "bad guy" in the ring is the local developer, a corporation using sweatshop labour, or even global capitalism itself. The "good guy" is the people, a local group, the Earth, to give a few examples. Maybe the referee is a journalist, trying hard to find a balance but always siding a little more with the bad guy. The announcer, maybe, is a newspaper or TV owner wetting his chops at the prospect of a spectacle. Because the owner gets paid in advertising,

---

* *Wikipedia: The Free Encyclopedia* ‹http://en.wikipedia.org›.

he will take steps to replace the referee if the ref sides too much with the good guy.

The battle can be summarized as: bad guy uses dirty tactics to start winning (throwing dust in eyes, paying off the referee, perhaps); just when it looks like all is lost, the people come together and overcome the bad guy to save the day. For the wrestling fan, picture Hulk Hogan in one of his patented frenzies overcoming anything that stands in his way.

WHY WRESTLING MATCH?

This action uses a cultural convention to convey a message, and it is also an effective way of representing a struggle, identifying an oppressor, and calling people together to work for a solution.

This is also a fun action to do and perform. It's about playing at wrestling—which many of us did with our neighbourhood crowd when we were kids, and which the WWE is all about (it's all performance rather than the real thing). This action is entertaining enough and potentially large enough that people will stop and watch it. The virtue of having a small crowd is that as soon as you get some people watching, you will probably draw in more—you get all the more ears for your message to reach.

WHAT YOU NEED

For this action you can go soft, medium, or hard core, depending on your available resources, people, and time. If you don't have much time, all you need is some string to create a square (your wrestling ring), actors (a referee, your bad guys and the good guys—who are, we would hope, not all guys), an announcer with a megaphone, and a script. If you have more time and resources, you can create a more formal ring (several old mattresses will do the trick), with makeshift posts and ropes, and you are ready to rumble.

The Power of Song

FUN ❄❄❄❄   RISK 0   RESOURCES 0

"SONG" IS ONE OF the most powerful unifying weapons we have. From the American civil rights movement to the labour movement to the Raging Grannies and local merry pranksters, there has always been song. "We Shall Overcome," "Solidarity Forever," "Swing Low Sweet Chariot," and "The Internationale" are among the best-known tunes in North America. There is something innately powerful in a good song that can't be captured in the two simple lines of the standard protest-march chant.

The 2001 FTAA negotiations in Quebec City saw large demonstrations, a huge People's Summit, and a tremendous police presence. For its part, FUNK (Fighting Unaccountable Naughty Korporations) used one van and two cars to take twenty-odd people from Edmonton to Quebec City. Most of the FUNK members were a little tired of the usual chants and protest rituals, and on the three-day drive to Quebec City we used walkie-talkies to write collective songs, sharing verses between the three vehicles. Eventually we came up with four songs. Picture twenty-two people in gas masks storming down the streets of Quebec, tear gas in the air, megaphones in hand, all singing "Come Join the Movement."

Come Join the Movement (to the tune of "The Ants Go Marching")

Come join the movement boys and girls,
It's fun, it's fun
We'll band together and get them
On the run, on the run
There's lots of us, and few of them
Don't let them get any REM
And we all go marching down around the wall again.

They say this is democracy
They're wrong, they're wrong
We say this is hypocrisy
We're right, we're right
Democracy, hypocrisy

It's all a friggin fallacy
And we all go marching down around the wall again.

Paul Martin is lying to you
For shame, for shame
Tony Blair is screwing you
Again, again
George Bush is using you
Get off your ass let's stage the coup
And we all go marching down around the wall again.

The gap between the rich and poor
It grows, it grows
We've got less and they've got more
It shows, it shows
Workers are being shown the door
Never forget what we're fighting for
And we all go marching down around the wall again.

Capitalism continues to thrive
Resist, resist
The revolution is coming alive
Enlist, persist
The issues at hand are black and white
Is there no end to this facist shite
And we all go marching down around the wall again.

The media say we're doing this
For kicks
THEY'RE PRICKS!
We're doing this 'cause the system needs
A fix
IT LICKS!
We won't give in to their demands
United we stand hand and hand
And we all go marching down around the wall again.

The reduction of our forests
Is a crime, a crime,
With carbon sinks depleting
All the time, all the time
Kyoto was a political joke
We want the president to choke
And we all go marching down around the wall again.

So come join hands with us today
Defend, my friend
We're fighting for our children's rights
For women, and men
As NAFTA drains our rights away
We hope you'll join with us this day
And we all go marching down around the leg again.

WHY THE POWER OF SONG?

Songs are a terrific way of contributing to a protest—they require no storage or upkeep, and they are inclusive. Anyone, young or old, rich or poor, can participate. Songs provide you with a way of getting your message across in a creative and listener-friendly way. It's a challenge to write a funny song—and the funnier, the better.

If you don't do anything else in this book, I encourage you to develop your own songs and sing them at the next rally. Take along sheets with the words printed on them to hand out. Then look at the people's faces as you pass by. People light up when they hear songs. Give them the words and they'll join.

WHAT YOU NEED

All you need for this action is an issue, a group of friends, and a tune. Access to photocopying helps too. Any songs that have easy lyrics and rhythm will work nicely. We have adopted everything from nursery rhymes and children's songs to the music of Twisted Sister. Songs with repeating choruses are good to use, because they allow people who don't have the words to join in. Action songs are also good, because it is all about drawing people in, including them, and the more ways you can find to do that, the better.

For easy North American songs, you can use "What Do you Do with a Drunken Sailor?" "She'll Be Coming Round the Mountain," or "If You're Happy and You Know It." These three are easy, they all have repeating verses, and you can develop actions to make them more participatory. Christmas carols are another easy starter.

Just sit down, brainstorm the issues you want to cover, and start writing. If you are really stuck, you can even just adapt our version of "Come Join the Movement"—we give you our full permission. You can change a few lines around in that one and make it relevant for pretty much any issue—we used it for an anti-war rally and an anti-tuition rally two days in a row.

When you have your song, practise it a few times and print up some sheets with the words so that other people can join in. This is one of the quickest actions you can do. Songs are the action that keeps on giving.

Mural Painting by Number

ACTION 38

FUN 🏃🏃🏃 | RISK ½ | RESOURCES 🎨🎨🎨½

CHANGE FOR CHILDREN is an Edmonton-based organization that works with children in Latin America. Their latest endeavour is a mural project in which they work with inner-city youth and use art to bring about change. I had the pleasure of working with Mario, one of the youth from Change for Children. I met him when student groups across North and South America were organizing against the GATS/FTAA negotiations, the next round of meetings in Quito, Ecuador, and Canada's involvement in the entire process.

Mario came to one of our meetings with the idea of doing a mural as his form of expression against the talks. Everyone loved the idea, but if it was to become a true community project, how could others get involved? The idea Mario came up with was perfect. The "artists" would work with us to produce an overall design for a painting. We would break the drawing down into pieces by basic colour, very similar to the paint by numbers type of art that many of us remember from our childhoods. From that point on, people could simply drop by the site, pick up a paintbrush, and fill in the blank pieces of the mural.

We purchased paint and brushes. Then, using a wall in the students' union building, our whole group, working together, came up with a general design and outline for the mural. The artists working with us divided the drawing into sections and identified the colours for each section. After that, at any one time two to twelve people worked on various pieces of the mural painting, and it was pretty much finished within a week. Everyone who worked on it not only had a fun time but also experienced the feeling of making a statement that would last well beyond the campaign.

WHY MURAL PAINTING BY NUMBER?

This action has very much the same rationale as the power of song (Action 37). Artists have an integral place in the struggle for a better world. Their tools have the ability to cut to the core of the issues and—just as important—to draw people into the discussions.

Painting by numbers extends the artist's function to the community. It gives everyone the power and skill of the brush. This action helps to build community. It creates a lasting image and gives people a chance to participate—what more can you ask for?

WHAT YOU NEED

First, you need to come up with an idea for a visual statement—the drawing. In doing this it is important to work with the larger community so that everyone has ownership over the entire process and the final product.

Once you have an idea for the artwork, you need one or two people who have the ability to draw the outline and divide the drawing into sections. To avoid mistakes you can start with a small-scale model that the participants can use as a guide when they start to work on the actual surface. Using an overhead projector to reproduce the small drawing on the wall makes things that much easier.

Then it is off to the paint store, or perhaps—especially if you are lucky enough to have an eco-station—you can get donated or free paint. You might have to adjust your design to the colours you manage to get.

With the paint and paintbrushes in hand and the basic design on the wall, all you need are volunteers to come out on the appointed day. Put a thick border of tape around the outline of the drawing so that you have a nice finished edge, and then everyone can just fill in the blanks.

After the art is finished, you could have some sort of unveiling and put up a small plaque to let people know what the mural represents and why it's there. A volunteer appreciation potluck is also a good way of solidifying the community that you have just drawn together.

Good luck and good painting.

Garden Car

FUN 🥾🥾🥾 | RISK ⚠ to ⚠ ⚠ ⚠ ⚠
depending on location | RESOURCES 👕 👕 👕 👕 👕

THIS IS AN ACTION inspired by a photo on the cover of a *National Geographic* magazine. The picture, taken in Tanzania, showed a broken-down car filled with soil and turned into a garden. Planting a garden in a car is one of the best reclaim the streets actions a person could do (see Action 9). The 1980 Toyota Corolla that a bunch of us have been driving for years is now on its last legs, and when it finally gives out my friends and I hope to place it in a strategic location, fill it with bags and bags of soil, and plant some seeds and a sunflower in it.

WHY GARDEN CAR?

Reclaiming the streets is always a good form of action, and that's what this one is all about. We live in a car culture—it is difficult, if not dangerous, to ride a bike on the streets of major cities, and we lose trees and green space to roadways on a daily basis. Our natural environment is being gobbled up, all to enable us to move faster and consume more goods. Most of the time old cars end up in the scrap heap or dump, where they further pollute our landscape. The garden car attempts to

create a lasting resistance to the car culture by turning one of the greatest destroyers of our time into something that can produce life.

The power of a single symbol can help change how we look and think about the world around us. Seeing "junk" as a possible life-producer can help us think about working to build the world we want to live and play in. A garden car takes a heap of metal destined for the scrap heap and turns it into something useful.

WHAT YOU NEED

This action is one of the most resource-intensive actions in this book because for it to work you need to get your hands on an old car or vehicle of some sort—and in particular a broken-down vehicle that otherwise no longer serves a useful purpose. When you have a vehicle that is no longer roadworthy (and in activist circles, for some reason, these cars do exist more often than not), take out all the useable parts and get ready to get dirty. Now you need soil, lots and lots of soil—enough to fill your car or vehicle to the window level. You need to pile the soil high, to make sure that people going by will be able to see your beautiful creation.

If you want to be especially labour-intensive, you can cut off the roof of the vehicle. This will increase exposure and allow your plants to feel the effects of more sunlight and even some rain. Of course, if you leave the top on your car you should also leave all the windows rolled down— or take them out completely. That way the plants can grow out the windows and get more sun and greater visibility.

Now you need to find a location. Where you put the car depends on how big a statement you want to make, how risky you feel, and how long you want your garden to last. If you want to make a big statement, and don't mind taking a risk, and don't care too much about how long your garden stays in place, then a roadway is ideal for you. Tow the vehicle out, fill it with pre-mixed soil and a few well-placed, already grown flowers, and in less than five minutes you are on your way. If you are more concerned about the longevity of your plants or seeds, or even the longevity of your message, then placing your creation on your own—or a friend's—property may be your best bet. Consider making the car part of your own backyard garden or lawn. This gives you more control, and the car is less likely to be seized. Get a group of guerrilla garden volunteers to help you with all of this.

Whether it is in the quick or the long-lasting location, planting already-grown flowers or plants lets people know immediately that your car is a garden and not just a car full of dirt. If your car is in a vulnerable location, make sure that you remove any identifiers, or you could find yourself responsible for the cost of hauling it away and possibly more. If it is in a secure location make sure that you look after your garden. Keep it nice, set up a schedule, and put your love into it.

40 ACTION

Singing Trees

FUN ❀❀❀½   RISK ½   RESOURCES 🌱🌱

SOMETIMES WHEN you do actions it's good not to do them as "people," but to do them as other beings.

We did this, for instance, when the G8 met in Kananaskis, Alberta, and the Canadian military decided that to ensure security they needed to build a perimeter fence—which in turn meant cutting down several trees and putting a fragile ecosystem at risk. That was when the idea of the singing trees was born. As Jean Chrétien pulled into the convention centre for a Liberal meeting, the singing trees were there in force. A couple of dozen trees sang beautiful songs to try to stop the Liberals from cutting their friends down. The trees also presented a petition signed by over three hundred different species of trees, all urging the Liberals not to destroy the natural environment along with the rest of the world.

WHY SINGING TREES?

Unfortunately, we live in a world that simply refuses to hear the call of nature. Every day dozens of species vanish from our world forever. Trees are being cut down and the natural environment is being polluted and destroyed at a rate unparalleled in the Earth's history. Most of us, by our actions, refuse to live within our means. Since no one can hear the screaming of our natural environment, we need to speak for the trees.

This action, in a very simple way, seeks to disturb the dominant worldview that the world is somehow just there for us—for human beings—that we are its masters rather than members of a complex web of relations.

WHAT YOU NEED

This is a difficult action when it comes to outlining the necessary resources because it could be done in so many different ways. The sky, or your imagination, is the only limit. To do the action of speaking for the trees, the prop list is fairly simple: a long petition with the signatures of various trees (for animals, paw prints would be appropriate), a few songs, and tree costumes. The tree costumes we used were cardboard cutouts painted forest green.

With props in hand, all you need are enthusiastic participants and an appropriate location to make your statement.

Corporate Whore

FUN ⚙⚙⚙⚙½   RISK ⚠   RESOURCES 🔦🔦🔦

I NEED TO APOLOGIZE right off the bat for the name of this action because it takes the word "whore" and uses it in a pejorative manner. Inga Muscio, author of *Cunt: A Declaration of Independence,** has clarified the word and its true, empowering meanings. Muscio uses a chapter on whores to show us that women who give, trade, and teach men about sexuality and what it means to be sexual are fulfilling an ancient—and what should be a respected and revered—role in our culture.

This action takes up a complex subject. It uses words and images that are usually socially constructed in a way that takes power away from women, woman-identified persons, and transgendered people. Again, the basis of this action is to take a culturally recognized symbol—the whore—and use that symbol to communicate something about the world we live in. This action should only be performed by feminists. It is important that your group members are conscious of how they are subverting/performing the kind of femininity capitalist that patriarchy has constructed as being okay for men to purchase.

"Corporate Whore" was created by Haley Dawn Nelson, a member of EARTh. It was performed during the federal election campaign, when Stockwell Day of the Canadian Alliance came to town for a fundraising dinner and speech. The action was essentially responding to the amount of money that corporations donate to political parties and candidates.

We put up a small circus tent outside the meeting hall and placed a hat on a table outside the tent, with a sign that said, "Donations Welcome." When a delegate to the Alliance dinner walked by, one of our

* Seattle, Wash.: Seal Press, 1998.

group would toss a quarter into the hat. The doors of the tent would open, and a man would step out, dressed in a fake fur coat and a Stockwell Day mask. When "Stockwell" was fully out of the tent, the fur coat would drop to the floor and reveal corporate symbols painted all over Stock's scantily clad body. The fake Stockwell would do a little dance, then pick up his fur coat and disappear back inside the tent until another coin would drop.

WHY CORPORATE WHORE?

Until 2003, when the situation became too transparently gross even for the ruling federal Liberal Party to stomach, corporations and wealthy individuals footed most of the bills for the pro-business political parties. The private sector wants a political process that deals with issues from its point of view, and as a result at election time the real choices get watered down beyond recognition—and it doesn't seem to matter who you vote for—big business always wins. This action calls into question the whole notion of corporate donations to political campaigns, and there is no more fun way to do this than by putting a man in a dress.

WHAT YOU NEED

The first thing you need is a tent or something you can hide your corporate dancer in until show time—tarps or even a refrigerator box will work. When you have your tent you now need a man—and it should be a man for this action—who is willing to dance and get his body painted. If you have time, do some research into the corporations that are lurking in the political shadows and come up with their logos. Banks and oil companies are the usual suspects. Get some body paint and get to work.

Get a mask of the politician you are seeking to represent. Or find a photo of his (less often her) face, blow it up, paste it on some cardboard, and use a string to keep it on. Find a fake fur coat or an overcoat, a hat, work out some snazzy dance moves, and you are ready to move on down the line.

Lobbying

| FUN 0 | RISK 0 | RESOURCES 👤👤 |

YAWN. LOBBYING IS the act of persuading legislators or other policy-makers to change an existing law or policy, create a new one, or reject a proposed change. Lobbying can be done at the municipal, provincial, or federal levels, and the techniques used at each level are fairly simple.

In my experience, politicians pay most attention to those who a) are from their constituency, b) represent a specific community of interest, group, or business, c) have donated to their campaign, and d) have public opinion behind them. As individual citizens we don't usually have the money to *really* influence a politician. One of the only effective ways of lobbying for change is by showing that you have public support behind you. Most politicians' thoughts are confined to their own reputations, influence, or popularity, and about their chances in the next election. By linking your voice to a larger voice outside the room, you have a better chance of influencing a decision.

That being said, I don't have a lot faith in the success of lobbying on anything more than *minute, mostly inconsequential* changes to legislation. In 2003 the University of Alberta students were facing a 6.9 per cent increase in tuition and University of Calgary students were facing a 6.4 per cent increase. After intense lobbying, combined with a tuition campaign that saw over sixty people sleep in tents in minus-thirty-five-degree weather in Edmonton, and one hundred people sleep in tents in Calgary, as well as rallies in both cities, the university boards of governors still voted in favour of the increases. At the University of Calgary the Students' Union even tried to reduce the increase by 0.1 per cent—which was also rejected by the board.

WHY LOBBYING?

If lobbying is usually not effective, why do it? Two reasons. The first is because change is sometimes possible through lobbying when it comes to small issues. Politicians are always trying to keep everyone happy, and if there is something small they can do to get you to go away with a smile, they are likely to do it. If something can be changed simply by lobbying, then that is the best way to go—your values will be reflected in law or policy.

When it comes to more fundamental changes, you will most likely be pitted against someone who is lobbying on the other side of the issue, and who almost certainly has more resources and money than you can ever hope for. This makes your job more difficult and the need for public support a necessity. A good argument can only take you so far.

The second reason for lobbying is a matter of perception. Politicians and the media are always trying to find ways of dismissing activists. Politicians can easily write you off by saying, "I was never even approached on this issue—that's the trouble with these people, all they ever do is complain, they never want to work with the system." This argument resonates among a general public that has never tried to change the system. The best way of counteracting this claim is by being able to say that you tried absolutely everything you could before you took to the streets. Being able to say that you lobbied, wrote letters, collected petitions—and still your voice fell on deaf ears—can help later on to draw in the sympathy, or at least the understanding, of the people who are now watching you lock your body to a gate to prevent a wetland from being paved over.

WHAT YOU NEED

The first thing you need when lobbying is to identify who you should be talking to. Who can actually make the changes I want? Is there a committee that this bill will go through first, and who sits on it? Is there someone in government who can be our champion on this issue, or who has spoken in favour of this issue in the past? Who are the staff members who advise the minister on this issue?

By identifying the people who are most likely to support your cause, you cut down on frustration and time. By taking a look at the minutes of whatever body you are targeting, you can see how members voted or spoke. Minutes are usually available on government websites. Mainly, you want to find a champion, someone within government who may be willing to take your issue and push for it. At the provincial and federal level, this is usually someone in cabinet, because they have the power to influence government decisions. If you can find a champion you are definitely on your way. Standing policy committees and caucus committees are often geared towards specific issues, such as housing or education. The politicians who sit on these committees sometimes have a higher degree of expertise in your policy area and may actually care about your concerns.

Another way of finding out who you should be targeting and how you should approach them is through the opposition parties—especially if they are more progressive than the government. Opposition researchers and policy people know the government, and they can often point you to members who think independently, or who are particularly influential.

Locate the minister or city councillor who is in charge of your issue. Set up a meeting with the people who advise the politician—the bureaucrats. These people are usually more friendly, more sympathetic to your cause, and freer to give you information and techniques on what may work with the politician in question.

Once you find out who to talk to, you should put together a short written submission outlining the issues, the reasons you are concerned, and the solutions to the problem. Politicians will miss a majority of what you say in a meeting, so a hard copy of your argument ensures that you deliver all the necessary information. The politician, or an executive assistant, can read your take on the issue later on if they ignored you during the meeting.

When you have your document ready, set up a meeting. Don't be intimidated. State your opinion, try to engage the politician in questions to get their feedback, and try to get some sort of commitment from them—raising a question in question period, raising the issue in cabinet or at a particular committee, or even proposing an amendment to a piece of legislation.

Next, follow up. Call the politician, and ask about the progress around the issue. Meet with other members who are on the same committee. Meet with the opposition and get them to raise questions in the House. Also, try to get a meeting with whoever represents your constituency.

If all else fails, proceed to the other actions listed in this book.

Letter–Writing, Petitions, and Writing Ladders

FUN 0	RISK 0	RESOURCES 🎫🎫

LETTER-WRITING AND petition campaigns are relatively easy and common actions and have been done so much that I don't want to insult my readers by dwelling on them. I will breeze over them and focus mostly on writing ladders, which may be less well known.

Writing ladders is a tool I first learned about when I was doing a campaign against government cuts to education. We had a group of people who were concerned about the issue, but weren't into visual or theatrical actions. They were writers. They would sign petitions and write letters, and that was the line in the sand. We needed to find a way past this resistance and turned to an established association for help. They told us about the writing ladder, and it worked perfectly.

We put together a list of forty volunteers willing to write letters to the editor. A person was appointed to scan the paper on a daily basis and look for education-related articles. Our goal was to raise the profile of post-secondary education. Every time an education-related article appeared in the paper, the co-ordinator phoned the first four people on the list. To ensure a cohesive message our group provided basic guidelines and asked them to write letters to the editor, in their own voices. Some of the letters ended up being published.

The next time an article appeared, the next four people were contacted, and so on, until eventually we got back to the beginning of the list.

A writing ladder can be set up to cover any basic issue.

WHY LETTER-WRITING, PETITIONS, AND WRITING LADDERS?

Petitions and letter-writing—like lobbying—are not the most effective ways of addressing large issues, but are a good way of getting people involved, of taking immediate action. They can be moderately effective in showing public support for an issue, and that can only help in other lobbying efforts. They are especially effective as a response to smaller issues.

Writing ladders are absolutely great for raising the profile of an issue. Each time a number of people write letters to the editor on the same issue, and those letters get published, you get a page of free advertising. Usually, the media spin on an issue is something that is hard to control. But with your letters to the editor you control the spin. You communicate the details you want the public to know. You can also sometimes get away with publicizing your events in a letter.

The other beauty of the writing ladder is that it allows people who aren't comfortable taking more confrontational actions a place to put their voices to good use.

WHAT YOU NEED

Letter-writing. All you need is the address of the person in charge of making the decision for the issue you are working on, plus a pen (or computer) and a piece of paper. To make it easier for other people to join in, or if you want to blitz a person with letters, it is good to have a small backgrounder or fact sheet, complete with the appropriate names and addresses of the targets, which you can then hand out to people. A sample letter is also a good idea—either as a guide, or for people to sign and send. If you are more web-savvy, you can set up an instant fax on your website, enabling visitors to send a fax with one click.

Petitions. Depending on where you are sending the petition, there are usually regulations you need to follow in order for it to be valid. This is true for provincial, federal, and municipal governments. You will find all the rules and regulations on government websites.

Writing Ladder. For a writing ladder, you need a list of interested people. It may be a good idea to hold an introductory session in order to brief everyone on the issues and the main points that you want to communicate. You need to appoint one or two co-ordinators who phone people and monitor the papers. When you have done that, you are pretty much ready to roll. This action is not at all time-consuming for your volunteers—if you have forty volunteers on the list, they will only have to write one letter every ten times the issue comes up in the media.

Create a Zine

FUN ❄❄❄½   RISK ½   RESOURCES ♟♟♟½

ZINES HAVE BEEN around since forever. One group of revolutionary women known as the True Wimmin Against Totalitarianism (or the T.W.A.T. team) uses zines to spread their feminist message far and wide. The zine, *T.W.A.T. Team News*, has articles on everything from stripping to local, provincial, and national politics, from songs and poetry to tips for organizing, and T.W.A.T. team merchandise. The group is completely anonymous and articles are submitted via e-mail. When enough articles are submitted to make up thirty pages, three T.W.A.T. team members get together and assemble it. They draw illustrations, or find pictures that they can use, and then photocopy the final pages. The group makes hundreds of copies and distributes them to bookstores, libraries, and all sorts of public places.

WHY CREATE A ZINE?

Punk rock musician and activist Jello Biafra says "don't hate the media — be the media." One easy way that people have used to accomplish that seemingly unreachable goal is to produce a zine. Zines can be your way of communicating your message with the world. Most of the actions in this book allow you only to get a sound bite to the outside world. Zines allow you to get your full message out, uninterrupted in full colour with as much detail and illustrations as you want. You control the spin, the distribution, everything.

Making a zine can be a great community-building activity. A group collects or writes articles, and argues over and decides on placement. The members edit, illustrate, and are in charge of circulation. The process is the same as in a big newsroom, only on a smaller scale. Working with people from beginning to end helps bring people together through the sharing of skills and gifts.

WHAT YOU NEED

Here is a list of seven questions that should help you to determine the type of zine that you want to produce and also, perhaps, help you focus your action. The list is from the article "Write a Zine That Doesn't Suck," found on the Vanity Press website **‹www.angelfire.com/on/vanitypress/ articles/zineact.html›**.

#1. Do you want to publish a web zine or a print zine? I would say that web-zines are much easier, cheaper to produce (thanks to free hosting like Angelfire and Geocities), and have more potential to be visually stunning, depending on your HTML expertise. With print zines you're pretty much limited to cut-and-paste, unless you have a really good computer and an inkjet printer. Cut-and-paste, I should warn you, is a tedious pain-in-the-ass process where glue stick eats your nail polish and little ribbons of text stick on your clothes and your butt and anywhere but where you want them to stick (i.e. the page). Meditate on this most important question for a while.

#2. Are you doing this by yourself? Going it alone is incredibly brave. Since you are probably nervous about getting enough ideas, you might want to enlist two or three friends to help you. Even asking just one friend for help automatically doubles your resource pool ("resources" = ideas and money, things no zine can do without). The downside of this is the inevitable power struggles that ensue (which, incidentally, is what led to the downfall of the zine I worked with . . .).

#3. Do you know what kind of zine you want to do? Maybe a general review/rant zine, or devote the whole thing to one thing/person (i.e. a "fanzine")? Some good places to go if you're stuck for ideas are New Pollution: HOW to write a zine and Lisa RC's amazing study of Writer's Block.

#4. Are you familiar with your market? A common complaint about indie zines is that a lot of them are very much alike. To survive more than a few issues, you'll need a different slant—not just random six-month-old movie reviews and "Why my life sucks" editorials. I recommend reading a lot of zines—visit Factsheet 5 Web Edition for a comprehensive overview—and listing what you like and don't like about each of them. Then accen-tu-ate the positive, as Thumper told Bambi. Or was that one of the mice in *Cinderella*?

#5. Are you rich? You don't necessarily have to be, but distribution and production depend on cash flow. I recommend getting a job somewhere where you have access to a copy machine—it will cut waaaaay down on costs. Seepage cut a deal with Mail

Boxes Etc. but they revoked the discount and asked us to stop advertising them due to our, uh, "mature subject matter" (as if we weren't providing a valuable service by printing Claudia's article on her first trip to the gynecologist). If you can't get unlimited access, find someone who does have it and befriend them. Ask them to write a column in exchange for copy privileges, and pray their writing isn't too awful. Most importantly, DON'T expect to make up the cost of production by charging like $5 for your zine . . . $1 is a good price. $2 only if it's really thick or is on glossy paper like the big boys have (mucho dinero for that, btw). I hope you can afford to lose some money every month . . . which brings us to . . .

#6. How often to publish? Seepage wanted to be monthly, but it was damn near impossible to keep up that pace amid school and work and sleep and five distinct and combative personalities. We switched to bimonthly and were much happier. There was more crucial breathing room. If you want to be monthly, start writing stuff now and always have one issue done or near-done a month in advance ("real" magazines work three months in advance) so you have enough time in case an emergency comes up. If you establish a fan base, you can't disappoint them by being inconsistent (a common problem in the world of zines).

#7. Do you *really* want to do this? Zine production eats time and money. You'll be competing against thousands of other zines almost exactly like yours. But if you really feel the world needs your distinctive outlook, as well as yet another Indigo Girls concert review, and you are possessed by the spirit of DIY ("Do it Yourself"—learn the lingo, now), by all means go for it. I don't want to discourage anyone from going after a dream (ahem, Mr. High School Guidance Counsellor who told me writing was a bad idea), but I want you to be aware of the inherent problems before you start.

Boxes of Apathy

FUN 🦋🦋🦋 ½ | RiSK ½ | RESOURCES 🎯🎯🎯

BOXES OF APATHY came out of a news report about a woman who was physically assaulted by her boyfriend in her apartment. The woman screamed for help but no one came—even though the building was full of people. This is a chronic problem in our society, where no one seems to want to "get involved" even when people are in distress. You may remember the story of a homeless man who froze to death right in the middle of downtown Toronto. You have probably witnessed instances where people ignore someone in distress yourself.

We live our lives in boxes that separate us from each other. The sense of community we had only a half-century ago is gone—we no longer feel connected to each other—and this action tries to capture this alienation. It starts with two boxes, both with actors inside and both open at the bottom so you can see their feet and they can move about. The actor inside Box A screams and pounds against the side of the box. The actor in Box B lifts the box a little (showing more legs) and shows concern by moving the box around a little, but essentially does nothing.

Box A then yells a little louder and pounds a little more. This time, Box B looks like it is going to do something, but instead elects to move away. Box A screams louder, B moves further away. Box A screams even louder and longer until eventually Box B turns and runs away, leaving A screaming. Eventually the scream turns to silence and then sobbing. At this point, two other actors come out with a banner that says something like "Violence against women is everyone's problem, speak out today," or "Oppression is a community issue, please don't turn your back."

This powerful action can evoke strong emotions in the audience, so use it with care.

WHY BOXES OF APATHY?

We need to start building communities. This action forces people to think about their own personal actions in everyday life. It can also make us think about our society's general state of immense denial. It is a sick society when one-quarter of the women in it will be physically assaulted in their lifetime, yet no one bats an eye. Our society rapes its children, its women, its trees, and the earth. We need to start dealing with this violence.

The action can be used as commentary for a variety of issues. Whether it's violence against women, general oppression, or that people are sitting by while a valuable wetland is destroyed, "boxes of apathy" can help to bring people to thought, if not action.

WHAT YOU NEED

For this action to be successful, you need two boxes big enough to completely cover your actors but light enough to be easily moved and carried around. Refrigerator boxes are good for this; they are lightweight but big enough to hide inside.

Next, you need four actors: two to be in the boxes (one with a voice that carries), and two to hold the banner up at the end and ensure safety. It is important that the audience doesn't see more than the feet or legs of the actors in the boxes, because otherwise the illusion created will be destroyed. When the actors in the boxes are finished, they can have one of the other participants guide them out of sight. To cheat, they can also cut eyeholes in the boxes.

Last, you need lots and lots of practice. Show it to people you know and see if they get it.

Free Stores

FUN 💸💸💸   **RiSK** ½   **RESOURCES** 🎗🎗🎗🎗🎗

IN NORTH AMERICA FREE stores rose to prominence in the 1960s. They could be found throughout the United States and were concentrated in larger California centres. Anything and everything could be found in a free store, from clothing and pots and pans to mattresses and even the kitchen sink. Abbie Hoffman helped set up a free store with only one rule: you can't steal from the free store.

Free stores still exist today. Usually most of the goods found in them are secondhand and would otherwise be destined for the dump. Goods are donated by people or reclaimed from dumpsters and back alleys. One of the best places to find free-store materials is a garage sale, especially because garage sale rejects usually go to the dump.

People can drop by during store hours and take what they want. If they can, they leave something in exchange. Material donated is cleaned and washed and put out for other people to have, and it is all free, free, free.

WHY FREE STORES?

The primary reason for a free store is that in our Western society we already have too many things. Our houses, garages, closets are riddled with disposable consumer crap. At the same time it seems we always have things we need to get—a shirt, a bookshelf, a blender, whatever. Instead of carting your rejects off to the dump and going off to buy new stuff, you can use a free store as a place where you and your community can get what you want and need. Free stores are environmentally friendly—they reduce consumption and thus refuse.

Free stores are open to everyone regardless of income, and they help build community. A community of people can become involved in running the store, or even in making donations to or simply using the free store, and the place becomes somewhere people can come together in a very low-pressure way.

WHAT YOU NEED

To build a free store, and for it to actually work, you need a core group of people who are excited about the idea. Then you need to find a space—even someone's garage will do. You need a place to store your goods, before they are cleaned and ready for display, and another place to use as your actual free store.

Once you have your space and your volunteers, you need goods. First, get donations from the people in the group. If that is not enough to start, put notices calling for donations up in your community, or put out calls for donations through e-mail lists. You can go to garage sales when they are winding down and ask if you can haul away the stuff they don't want. Or you can drive down streets or back alleys and pick stuff up before it is taken away as garbage.

When you have enough stuff and have cleaned it properly (you don't want a lawsuit on your hands), you need to advertise your store's existence. You can do this by putting up posters in your community, going door to door, placing notices in community papers, or using lawn signs.

Finally, you need office hours. People like things to be reliable, so sporadic hours can work against you. But if you can only manage to put in sporadic hours, then that's what you have to do. A free store usually only requires one person at a time to supervise it, but needs a lot of people behind the scenes to clean, collect, do the displays, and so on. There is a lot of people-power required for a free store, but remember: just because something's free, doesn't make it easy. Democracy is free too.

Corporate Crime Fighters

ACTION 47

FUN 🐓🐓🐓🐓🐓 | RISK ½ *(without an aide)* | RESOURCES 🌲🌲½

EVERYONE, IT SEEMS, is fascinated with superheroes. North American children grow up with characters like Batman, Superman, Wonder Woman, Spiderman, Wolverine, and the Incredible Hulk. These characters speak to us, because they stand up for truth and justice in the face of great odds. Robin Hood is one of the all-time classic characters because he does what people feel is right, and necessary, by taking money from the rich and giving it to the poor. Children in particular have an intuitive response to this kind of superhero, given that their moral compass hasn't yet been jaded by years of capitalist indoctrination.

Mexico, for instance, has its Super Barrio Man, a masked man with a cape who sticks up for the poor and powerless and is therefore a Mexican legend. In North America we have Michael Moore's Crackers the Corporate Crime Fighting Chicken, who travels all over America bringing corporate criminals to justice. On TV in Canada comedian Mary Walsh and her character Marg the Princess Warrior has fearlessly confronted politicians and other bigwigs.

You too can have your own caped crusader and take back your own streets. We had our own giant chicken, Cookie the Corporate Crime Fighting Chicken, and accompanying him, as every good superhero has a sidekick, we had a six-foot gorilla named Gord. Cookie and Gord's first action was against our university's board of governors, which is made up of two groups—university administration and "public members" who are all representatives of corporations. One year, when the board was all set to raise tuition, our fearless crusaders burst into the meeting room. The looks on the faces of the stuffy, suited board members were worth the entire thing. The crusaders made gallant speeches about why the board had to lower tuition in the name of justice. The giant chicken presented a gravestone for accessible education to the chair of the board and shut the entire proceedings down. The action only lasted fifteen minutes, but the administration, students, and the board remember it to this day.

WHY CORPORATE CRIME FIGHTERS?

People like superheroes—they like having someone to root for, so you have an immediate measure of crowd support. Children especially love superheroes or mascots in costume, and their eyes just light up when they see Cookie, the giant chicken. When you have children in your corner, it is also much harder for security personnel to remove you. Just imagine how loud a child would scream if they saw Barney getting beat up by a police officer.

Superhero actions draw media attention. The cameras are all over giant gorillas and giant chickens, so if you structure it carefully, you can get your message out.

If you do enough superhero actions, people will come to expect you to show up in the struggle for justice. If you get to this point, you really have succeeded in becoming a superhero and are in the process of creating a legend.

The only caution here is that superhero imagery, like wrestling, is intensely gendered. The conventional metaphorical language privileges male strength, individualistic adventures, and bravado to communicate a message of good vs. evil. This means that you and the people you work with have to be critical enough of your own actions to recognize when you are using gender in a way that does not adequately critique the patriarchy. Female superheroes are therefore key, if you have a woman who is willing. If men dominate your group you should still consider having a female superhero—but then again, if men dominate your group you should probably be spending your time thinking long and hard about your commitment to social justice before you strike out in the name of the oppressed.

WHAT YOU NEED

To perform this action successfully, you need a super costume. It can be as little as a cape, or it can be a full costume; you just need something catchy and identifiable. A full costume is best, so that one individual doesn't have to be responsible for each and every action. Anyone can use our Cookie outfit, which enables the chicken to be absolutely everywhere.

After you have the costume, you have to think of ways of getting your message out. Most of the time newspapers will only take a photograph of you, and TV crews will take pictures, but there won't necessarily be sound, so you need to ensure that your message gets out—you need to make it so that you aren't just a chicken suit without any politics. To overcome this problem, our group used a fake gravestone. Our message was clearly printed on it, and the writing was big enough that it could be seen from a distance. You can use anything, as long as it has a readable message on it.

Another tip: you need to ensure that your audience doesn't see who is under the mask. Even if people think they know who that person in the suit is, they will still have doubts about it—this is the magic of costume, and the mystery adds to the action. If Spiderman simply went into action as Peter Parker, he would have very little success. The same is true for you—so keep your superpowers to yourself.

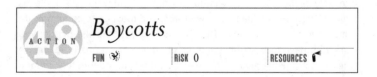

ACTION 48

Boycotts

FUN 🐥 | RISK 0 | RESOURCES 👆

THE WORD "BOYCOTT" goes all the way back to the late nineteenth century and a retired British army officer, Captain Charles Cunningham Boycott (1832–97), who took up a position as a land agent in Ireland's County Mayo. After a crop failure in 1879 his tenants couldn't pay their rents and were facing the possibility of famine. When the Irish Land League asked Captain Boycott to reduce his rents, he refused to do so and instead tried to evict the tenants. In 1880, on the advice of the Land League, the tenants decided to ostracize the land agent—they refused not just to pay their rents but also to harvest their crops or even to communicate with him. Captain Boycott ended up fleeing to England, where he eventually died in obscurity, but his name lives on, defined (by *The Canadian Oxford Dictionary*) as: "combine to coerce or punish (a person, company, nation, etc.) by a systematic refusal of normal commercial or social relations."

One of the more famous boycotts in North America occurred in Montgomery, Alabama, in the 1950s. Most people remember the name of Rosa Parks—her symbolic act of refusing to move to the back of the bus not only led to the Montgomery Bus Boycott by the Black community in 1955–56 but also sparked the larger civil rights movement in the United States, eventually leading to the change of segregation laws. But it took thousands of committed people, not just one Rosa Parks, to achieve that goal.

The United Farm Workers boycotts, begun in the 1960s by César Chávez, led to important changes in labour conditions. Boycotts against South Africa played a role in ending apartheid there. Another well-known boycott was the one against the Nestlé corporation, for hooking Third World women and their babies on instant formula. Studies showed that the rise of bottle feeding greatly increased the infant death rate in Third World countries. Boycott organizers also attacked the tuna industry, which was killing dolphins in its fishing practices. The campaigns against Nestlé and the tuna industry triumphed when the mega-corps changed their wicked ways—although Nestlé later reverted to its practices of promoting its baby milk—essentially killing babies for profit— and the campaign had to begin anew in the 1990s—which only suggests the need for constant vigilance.

The 1990s also saw the beginnings of a boycott campaign against Nike for its labour abuses in Vietnam and other Asian manufacturing operations.* By March 2000 *The New York Times* was announcing "the return of the boycott," stating: "Not since the 1970's, when grape workers and the anti-apartheid movement were holy causes for millions of Americans, have so many groups embraced the boycott as a weapon."

---

* Just type "Boycott Nike" into an Internet search engine and you'll come up with a list of many websites devoted to this issue.

These days, in addition to the campaign against Nestlé, I am participating in a number of boycotts: against the oil companies Shell (for its human rights record in Nigeria) and Esso (which actively denies global warming and has campaigned against the Kyoto Accord); against Wal-Mart and the Gap for their children's rights and sweatshop abuses; and, of course, the easiest one, against McDonald's, for its labour practices and fast food excesses in general.

This is by no means an exhaustive list. Boycotts are called and organized all the time, to varying degrees of effectiveness. Learning about them, following the issues, and then sticking to them call for more than a little perseverance.

WHY BOYCOTTS?

Boycotts can be an effective way of putting pressure on a business. If you get enough people to stop shopping at a store, eating at a fast-food joint, or buying products produced by a certain company, these outfits will start losing money and become more willing to address their errant behaviours. It's also very easy for people who support your cause to become involved in a boycott. It doesn't take a tremendous amount of effort to pass by a McDonald's and go to Wendy's instead. Especially when people have a real choice about whether to do business with a specific company or not, boycotts can be a successful way of getting your message across.

The only thing a corporation cares about is its bottom line. When profits start dropping, shareholders get angry and things change. This is the power we have. Boycotts don't require us to get together or hold meetings—they only ask us to consume consciously. While this is not enough—after all, it allows us to continue our alienated little lives under capitalism without building alternative communities—small corporate changes brought about by consumer boycotts do matter.

WHAT YOU NEED

When organizing a boycott, you need to make sure that the store or company knows what's going on. A silent boycott doesn't work, because there are so many different reasons why a company could be losing money. Unless the corporation knows that the reason its market share is dwindling is because it uses rainforest lumber or exploits workers, it will never change. So you need to start by informing the target that if it won't negotiate with you, you will organize a boycott. The warning gives the company a chance to change its policy.

Once the boycott is in progress, have people tell the shopkeepers, managers, or CEOs why they aren't shopping there, or have people write letters to the company. If you are more courageous, you can get together with a bunch of other people and do an action in the store you are boycotting. Most companies are forced to report any disturbances to their higher-ups. By creating a disturbance, you can add to the effectiveness of your action and ensure that your concerns are registering at the management level.

The main task in organizing a boycott is to educate consumers so that they can change their buying habits. Posters, leaflets, picketing (near the store, but not on its property unless you are prepared to move when they tell you to, or risk arrest), and talking to people are all effective ways of doing education about your issue. The Internet is also a great tool. Posting a website with your concerns will let your message reach far and wide.

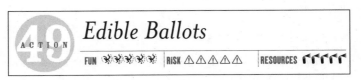

Edible Ballots

ACTION 49

FUN 🥄🥄🥄🥄🥄 RISK ⚠️⚠️⚠️⚠️⚠️ RESOURCES 📣📣📣📣📣

THE EDIBLE BALLOT SOCIETY (EBS) is a cross-Canada movement of people seeking to raise serious questions about the state of democracy in Canada. The EBS started in the federal election of 2000, when in various creative ways members of the group ate their ballots in polling stations across the country.

In Edmonton activists carried the necessary equipment and props into the polling stations, where they puréed their ballots in blenders, mixed them into stir-fries, and combined them in ballot sandwiches—although some participants just ate them raw. An eater enters the polling station just like any normal voter would, gets a ballot, and proceeds into the voting booth. In the booth, you rip off the part of the ballot with the Governor General's signature on it so you can take it back and deposit it in the ballot box (for counting purposes). You then make your statement on the floor of the polling station as you prepare and consume the rest of the ballot.

In the 2000 election across the country, over sixty people consumed or drank their ballots. In Edmonton five ballot eaters were eventually charged: three with destroying or defacing a ballot and two with interfering with the electoral process. The reasons for the discrepancy in charges are that the first three ate their ballots at an advanced poll (so that the action would get "maximum impact"). The other two charged ate their ballots on election day when the polls were packed with people. All five went to court. Elections Canada spent hundreds of thousands of dollars gathering evidence and preparing its case. Eventually all the charges were dropped and the Edible Ballot Society activists were finally free.

WHY EDIBLE BALLOTS?

It is fairly difficult to find anyone who thinks that the electoral process in Canada is fine and dandy. People either feel alienated from the process, powerless to change it, or feel that there is no one to vote for, only people to vote against. Being guilt-tripped into voting for the least offensive politician isn't synonymous with genuine democracy. Our electoral process is shallow—we don't have any real power to make decisions, just the illusion of democracy. Unless we press for real change, we will continue to jump from election to election, gradually becoming bored into submission. The Edible Ballot Society states its rationale on a TAO website ‹www.tao.ca›:

> It doesn't matter who you vote for, the government always gets in—the government being big business, and those who can afford to fund political parties or hire lobbyists. The elected

party is just the changeable mask on the face of corporate power.

Voting in this election is not only useless, it actually undermines democracy by giving legitimacy to prevailing power structures which are inherently undemocratic. Don't be guilt-tripped into voting for the least offensive party. Vote your desires and destroy your ballot.

Voting is really an insignificant act compared to the greater goal of creating authentic democracy. We need to participate in forging real communities through everyday acts of resistance and community building. A vote every couple of years is not democracy, it's repressive. Get over it.

It is true that voting should not be taken lightly or for granted, but the struggle for democracy should not end once we are given the vote. We need more than the illusion of democracy. We need to continue our resistance and defiance so that we all have power.

Most of us—even if we agree with several of the tenets of the EBS—never take the time to ask the basic questions about democracy or to build structures to enhance how it works. Eating your ballot creates an event that provides enough space for the questions to be asked. After eating at the advance polls and alerting the media, members of EBS used the coverage to organize forums to discuss the state of democracy in Canada. Letters and e-mails poured in, letters to the editor were written (pro and con the action), and forums on democracy popped up across the country. Questions that had to be asked finally were being asked and discussed from sea to sea to sea, which was one of the main purposes of the action in the first place.

WHAT YOU NEED

It doesn't take much to become a member of the Edible Ballot Society. Simply find a group of people who feel the same way and get ready. (See the group's suggestions, including a sample recipe, reprinted here from its website.) The only other suggestion I have is that if your goal is to get media coverage, you should do the ballot-eating at the advance polls, because otherwise any message you want to deliver will itself be eaten up by election coverage on the big day—and there will be less chance of "interfering with the electoral process."

You might want to contact a lawyer who is willing to defend you, just in case you get into some legal hassles. The bigger the media splash the more likely a lawyer will be willing to donate her or his services. All legal costs for the EBS were pro bono.

If your main purpose is to build democratic structures, start to prepare public forums in advance but don't announce them until the press picks the action up. The public forums are what makes the action more significant, because they provide an opportunity to raise awareness and build consensus around working to create a more democratic world. At the very least they can help to move the discussion along.

In some cases, for people who decide that they simply must vote in order to exercise their democratic option—but who feel they get themselves dirty in the process—the EBS has set up washing stations outside the polling place.

The Goal: Destroying Your Ballot

When you receive your ballot from the poll clerk, be careful. Hold the ballot gingerly between two fingers. If it moves, drop it immediately and step on it. If its stench bothers you, plug your nose. Examine the ballot. If you feel overwhelmed by the vast array of choices, then you are not at a polling station, you are in a supermarket. If the prospect of voting in this bogus democracy is repulsive, ask for another ballot. You are entitled to it under the Canada Elections Act. Is the second ballot better? If it is, you are either on medication or the poll clerk is playing a joke on you. If it isn't, you have no option but to put the thing out of its misery.

There are many ways to destroy a ballot. You can choose one of many options. As with voting, it doesn't matter what you choose, the end result is the same—your ballot gets destroyed. The choice is superficial, but you may as well choose a method which best suits your style and wardrobe.

Here are some suggestions:

1) Rip it

2) Burn it

3) Use it as toilet paper
4) Roll it into a huge joint and smoke it
5) Eat it
6) Fold it into a crane
7) Fold it into a paper airplane and fly it out the window
8) Shove it up your nose
9) Dissolve it in acid
10) Make confetti out of it
11) Fold it into a dish (use it for peanuts, soy nuts, or as an ashtray)

Our favourite method: EATING YOUR BALLOT

The trick to cooking with ballots is to use lots of strong spices. This will mask the bitter taste of big business and money. As always when handling ballots, make sure to wash your hands thoroughly with soap and hot water. If you are concerned about coming into contact with the germs of corporate power, you might want to wear latex gloves.

Note: The Surgeon General warns that ballots are toxic and can be hazardous to your health. Eating one every four years probably won't kill you, but putting one in the ballot box probably will.

Our favourite recipe: Jonnie's Ballot Burger with a side order of Literature de Campaign.

If the ballot is not yet dead, kill it. This can best be accomplished by hitting it repeatedly with a baseball bat or large stick.

• Deep-fry the ballot for one hour in a light cooking oil. This will ensure that all bacteria is killed. Add plenty of garlic and hot peppers, then the onions and cook under low heat for five minutes salting lightly.

• Next add mushrooms and fresh ground pepper and cook for two more minutes.

• Throw the mixture onto a bun and garnish with lettuce, tomatoes, and pickles.

• Slather the bun with plenty of ketchup, Dijon mustard, and secret sauce. If secret sauce is not available at your local supermarket, you can find it in any government department or ministry.

• Marinade the campaign literature in olive oil, basil, tarragon, salt, pepper and garlic. Apply the marinade liberally . . .

• The campaign literature should be grilled for at least five hours to ensure that it is edible. Even then, you probably won't be able to swallow it, but it is better to swallow it than actually read it.

• If you smell burning, don't worry. This is what you are aiming for.

• After your meal, be sure to gargle. The aftertaste from your meal can be fatal. Some people gargle with salt water, but battery acid does a more thorough job.

Mock Awards

ACTION 50

FUN ❄❄❄❄ | RISK ⚠ | RESOURCES 👆👆

"ON BEHALF OF the people of Canada, I would like to congratulate you on being one of the worst sweatshop abusers in the world."

With those words we presented the inhumanitarian of the year award to the manager of the Gap. We were all dressed in suits, as it was a big occasion. The men even wore corsages. We brought our own crowd to cheer and our very own photographer for the big moment.

We proceeded into the store. Our appointed announcer immediately made her way to the middle of the store and started the ceremony by calling attention and telling prearranged cheesy jokes. She welcomed everyone and then introduced the award presenters, who came up and read the list of nominees: the Gap, Hudson's Bay, Wal-Mart, and Victoria's Secret. "And the winner is . . . the Gap."

By that time the store manager had been alerted and she emerged from the back to tell us that Security was on the way. Not to be distracted, one of our presenters grabbed the manager's hand, shook it, and gave her the award—posing just for a second for a great photo-

graph. After delivering the award and passing out our handbills—which outlined the reason for the award—we packed up and left, with another successful action behind us.

WHY MOCK AWARDS?

There are already too many award shows that mean next to nothing, so it is about time we had one that actually carried some meaning. This show operates on the same premise as a boycott; that is, the best way to bring about corporate change is to do something that has an impact on a company's bottom line, making people aware of the company's dismal, destructive record. Whether the award is for the best polluter, the number one corporate criminal, or the biggest community destroyer, the result is an embarrassment for the company and a heightened awareness of your issue. If you combine a mock award with a boycott, you can double your effectiveness.

Mock awards are also a lot of fun. Unlike many actions that focus on the negative, this one is sarcastically positive. The media will also tend to jump on this type of event, because it gives them the visuals they are looking for, combined with a very simple message.

WHAT YOU NEED

Depending on whether you want to catch people by surprise or you want to put on a real show, the amount of backup needed changes. You definitely need something you can present as an award—even an old bowling trophy will do—and some literature explaining your action. Other than that, your props will depend entirely on the situation. If you are trying to give an award to George W. Bush for executing great numbers of people in the state of Texas—beating out other capital punishment aficionados in places like Libya and China—you should probably proceed cautiously and quietly and, especially, dress like the people you will be around. Then you just might have the best possible chance of getting close enough to give him the award. But if the target person does not have tight security control, and one of the main focuses of your action is getting the message out to the public, then the more hoopla the better.

Dress in costume, get a few people, go over a script, and run through possible scenarios. The more you practice, the better off you are for unforeseen situations. What if a security guard comes? What if the manager is irate? What if they try to ignore you or nobody pays attention? These are all questions that you have to think about and prepare for.

Occupations

FUN ❄❄❄❄ | RISK △△△△ ½ | RESOURCES 👤👤👤 ½

IN THE WAKE OF September 11, 2001, governments all over the world started introducing new legislation designed to protect us against "terrorism." In Canada proposed bills offered definitions of terrorism so vague and broad that they seemed designed to thwart legitimate political dissent and protests, like the one against the G8 Summit in Kananaskis, Alberta, in June 2002.

Initially at least, Canada's proposed "anti-terrorism" legislation would have allowed police to detain people without reason for up to seventy-two hours, to declare any area (for instance, the location of the 2002 Summit) a military zone and to institute military law. It would have allowed the federal government to seize the assets of any group suspected of being involved in terrorism (without ever being proven in a court of law). These groups would then be added to a government list. To get off the list and have their assets "un"-frozen, the group in question would have to go through a three- year court procedure. The government would also have expanded power to withhold information from the public. The proposed legislation would see Canada's Charter of Rights and Freedoms severely compromised, circumventing civil rights in the name of security. All in all, in the winter after 9/11, in response to enormous pressure from the Americans to be seen as "fighting terrorism," Canada's draconian "anti-terror" legislation was being rammed through Parliament.

The justice minister at the time was Anne McLellan, who, conveniently for us, represented an Edmonton constituency. So thirty of us decided something needed to be done. With very little time to organize, we decided to do an occupation and take over her office, located in a small building in the city's west end.

At eleven o'clock on a Friday morning—equipped with backpacks, food, and sleeping bags—we piled into her office, going past the front reception area to a back section that had two meeting rooms as well as cabinets containing the MP's files. There we sat ourselves down. We apologized to the staff for the inconvenience and explained that we meant no harm—we tried to make it clear that we believed the "anti-terror" legislation was so important that we needed to do something to protect fundamental freedoms in Canada.

Within the hour the police arrived, and so did the media. We grouped together and appointed members to work as media and police liaisons. The police liaison had no authority to speak for the group, only the authority to relay messages. She went to ask the police what they wanted, the media liaison went to speak to the media, and the rest of us settled in and started singing our prearranged songs, all having to do with the proposed legislation.

In the subsequent eight hours our police liaison would get demands from the police, bring them back to the group, and we would huddle together and decide what we could comply with and what we had to refuse. Our liaison would then take the results back to the police, get their feedback, and come back to convey the new demands to the group. This process repeated itself over and over again. *Hint:* this tactic buys you hours of time. Even if no one is willing to get arrested, you can still have an eight- to twelve- hour occupation because of the time it takes to negotiate.

Eventually we reached an agreement with the police. We would move out of the back part of the office and into the front reception area, on the condition that we could stay until Monday, at which time we would rene-gotiate. So now we were in for the weekend. The police were gone, although a security guard was positioned with us in the back office. With the police gone, the media also took off. We needed to come up with other ideas to draw attention. Thus each day we sat down and had a brainstorming meeting. No idea was too "out there." We settled on four sets of actions: a) conduct teach-ins every day to inform the community about the issues; b) have outside people go door to door in the area to tell the community what was going on; c) do an eviction action (move all the justice minister's stuff out onto the lawn in front of her office) on Saturday, and a funeral for civil liberties on Sunday; and d) come up with a list of demands.

In the three days of occupation we were able to garner tremendous community support—strangers brought us hot chocolate, cookies, and even sushi. The media gave us national exposure, and we were able to spawn three other occupations at different federal constituency offices in Canada. On Monday the cops came and prepared to move us out. By that time over two hundred people had gathered outside the office, and one hundred sat inside it.

The thing to remember with occupations (though this may not be true in all jurisdictions) is that before you can be charged with trespassing, someone with the authority to determine who can stay in the building needs to come to you, touch you on the shoulder, and specifically ask you to leave. *Until that point you cannot be charged.* In our case only eleven people stayed after the authorities came in to ask people to leave. But the police did not know that only eleven of the people in Anne McLellan's office were willing to be charged—all they knew was that there were one hundred people there, all potentially willing to be dragged out. Most of the time, law enforcement officers are not keen to drag people engaging in peaceful civil disobedience out of anyplace when there are TV cameras around to record it all—this is definitely one time when the corporate media are your ally.

The McLellan Eleven were charged with trespassing (the equivalent of a parking ticket; it does not stay on your permanent record). As it turned out the anti-terrorism legislation was passed into law, although amended slightly. But the risks of criminalizing peaceful activity and of unfair trials remained. Under a bill on public safety the armed forces could declare "controlled access zones" wherever military equipment is kept. In the end the charges against the McLellan Eleven were dropped.

WHY OCCUPATIONS?

A refusal to be "moved out" in an occupation is a major tactic in direct action. A group of people who simply refuse to be moved can do a lot of things. They can prevent trees from being cut down, missiles from being delivered, or an office or operation from running "efficiently."

You can never completely prevent yourself from being moved, but there are a lot of techniques that can help you stall for time, and sometimes stalling is all you need to perfect your action. Occupations can be legal or illegal depending on your level of risk. You can bring a lot of attention and community support to an issue and end up with little more than a parking ticket.

Occupations are high risk but carry the promise of high rewards as well. You can minimize your risks and still reap the rewards. For example, you do not need to see the occupation through to an arrest situation, and you do not need to escalate it—as we did by waiting for the eviction—in order to step up the media attention. But escalation does lead to loads of media attention, which means you increase your ability to get out your message and get the result you want.

WHAT YOU NEED

A group of dedicated people. Not everyone needs to be willing to get arrested, but the whole group must be prepared to stay and negotiate for as long as they can.

You should have a map of the place you intend to occupy. Whether you can get a real map or not, it's good to send a couple of people out to check out the venue. You should know where the washrooms are, whether or not the windows open, and where the exits are.

You need to ensure that you have enough supplies to stay for a good length of time—you might be there for a while. Even if you only plan on being there for a short time, conveying the illusion that you are going to stay for a week plays in your favour. Have lots of water and food. You need at least one cell phone you can use to contact media, lawyers, or even friends to feed your cat. (Remember also to bring along all the phone numbers you need). You may want to have video cameras, chains, locks, and mattresses as well (see also Action 52, Blockades).

Have one person in your group stay at home to help co-ordinate the group from the outside. This person should have a list of everyone involved, everyone's emergency contact information, and their personal requirements (medication, pets, etc.). After that, as with every action, ensure that the visuals convey your message. Be wary of where the cameras are pointed, and try to get your message or banner into every shot.

Blockades

FUN ❄❄❄   RISK ⚠⚠⚠⚠⚠   RESOURCES ☛☛☛☛

THE CLAYOQUOT SOUND region on Vancouver Island—a vast area of fjords and land comprising hundreds of nautical miles and a maze of off-shore islands—is home to the largest redwoods in the world and one of the largest rainforests left in the world. Over the last fifty years, 80 per cent of the area has been logged. But still the highway that goes into the area is one of the most beautiful roads in the world. Driving there you pass through densely wooded areas in which you feel as though you are in a different world. Huge, almost unimaginable trees line both sides of the road. The air smells different, animals are everywhere, and life in general seems peaceful. Eventually you come to a corner in the road, and you witness a devastating sight—you go from seeing some of the largest trees in the world to a dismal, complete clear-cut. After that, mile after mile is clear-cut forest.

In 1992, to stop the logging of the last remnants of the Clayoquot Sound forest, groups from all over North America gathered together to blockade the road. Using lock boxes, some of the activists locked themselves to a bridge near the town of Tofino, and they simply refused to move. As people got arrested and carted off, others would emerge and take their place. For years, the classic standoff took place between environmentalists and the loggers. Eventually the crusaders won their battle, and portions of Clayoquot Sound were protected. Still, as the Friends of Clayoquot Sound state in their website ‹www.focs.ca›:

> In January 2000, Clayoquot Sound was declared a UNESCO Biosphere Reserve. This designation does not offer any additional protection to the area, nor does it require the implementation of new environmental standards. Industrial logging continues to destroy the Sound's forests and fish farms continue to pollute its waters.

WHY BLOCKADES?

By blockading a road, you can prevent or delay something from happening. The action is more than a symbolic stand, because you are putting your body on the line and can actually help to bring about change.

The blockade is a very high-risk action—it can result in loggers yelling or revving their trucks at you. Angry workers and hostility are things that people need to be aware of and prepare for, but if done well, this action can reap high rewards.

WHAT YOU NEED

For any blockade, you have to take a number of important safety precautions. Always have a group of people in the action. Have one person or even two with video cameras to film all interactions with different groups—loggers, workers, police officers. The presence of video cameras can force people to act more cautiously, which is always in your best interest. It's also good to alert the media of your action, but you can't entirely depend on them to show up and provide safety.

Learn some de-escalation techniques to defuse hostile situations. Talk calmly and tell workers that you are sorry for disrupting or delaying their jobs. As in occupations, you should appoint police and media liaisons separate from the action to negotiate and help in tense situations. You should also try to forge good connections with the locals, especially Aboriginal people.

Sit-in and occupation techniques (see Action 50) can apply in blockades as well—they are a low- tech way of getting results. Simply linking arms with other protestors (or objects) can make it more difficult for people to remove you—which will make your action last longer and in turn give you more time to get your point across.

Often, police will use "pain compliance" of some sort—for instance, bending your wrists back—to force you to move. To prevent this, some protestors will use chains and a padlock or handcuffs or even use some more extreme method (such as a lock box) to fix themselves to something immoveable on the site, all to make life more difficult for the police. This sort of thing can require, at bare minimum, the police to get bolt cutters, a blow torch, or pliers to remove you. If you really do it well, a number of demonstrators can connect themselves together in a way that makes it practically impossible for them to be removed.

If you choose to do this type of action, make sure that someone else who is not locked in has the necessary key or other means of freeing you, in the event that you have to remove yourself quickly.

You may face legal action if you don't remove yourself when the police give you your final warning. But the consequences for not leaving are the same as for an occupation: a trespassing violation.

Appendix: Ten Commandments for Changing the World

by Angela Bischoff and Tooker Gomberg

CHANGING THE WORLD is a blast. It's all the more achievable if you have some basic skills, and lots of chutzpah. With apologies to Moses, and God, here are our top Ten Commandments for Changing the World. Try them out on your issue. Have fun!

But first, some inspiration from Noam Chomsky: "If you go to one demonstration and then go home, that's something, but the people in power can live with that. What they can't live with is sustained pressure that keeps building, organizations that keep doing things, people that keep learning lessons from the last time and doing it better the next time."

1. You Gotta Believe

Have hope, passion, and confidence that valuable change can and does happen because individuals take bold initiative.

2. Challenge Authority

Don't be afraid to question authority. Authority should be earned, not appointed. The "experts" are often proven wrong (they used to believe that the earth was flat!). You don't have to be an expert to have a valuable opinion or to speak out on an issue.

3. Know the System

The system perpetuates itself. Use the tools you have—the telephone is the most underrated. The Internet can be of great value for research as well. Learn how decisions are made. How is the bureaucracy structured? Who are the key players? What do they look like? Where do they eat lunch? Go there and talk with them. Get to know their executive assistants. Attend public meetings.

4. Take Action

Do something—anything is better than nothing. Bounce your idea around with friends, and then act. Start small, but think big. Organize public events. Distribute handbills. Involve youth. It's easier to ask for forgiveness after the fact rather than to ask for permission. Just do it! Be flexible. Roll with the punches and allow yourself to change tactics midstream. Think laterally. Don't get hung up on money matters; some of the best actions have no budget.

5. Use the Media

Letters to the editor of your local newspaper are read by thousands. Stage a dramatic event and invite the media—they love an event that gives them an interesting angle or good photo. Bypass the mainstream media with e-mail and the World Wide Web to get the word out about your issue and to network.

6. Build Alliances

Seek out your common allies, such as other community associations, seniors, youth groups, labour, and businesses, and work with them to establish support. The system wins through Divide and Conquer, so do the opposite! Network ideas, expertise and issues through e-mail lists. Celebrate your successes with others.

7. Apply Constant Pressure

Persevere—it drives those in power crazy. Be as creative as possible in getting your perspective heard. Use the media, phone your politicians, send letters and faxes with graphics and images. Be concise. Bend the administration's ear when you attend public meetings. Take notes. Ask specific questions, and give a deadline for when you expect a response. Stay in their faces.

8. Teach Alternatives

Propose and articulate intelligent alternatives to the status quo. Inspire people with well thought- out, attractive visions of how things can be better. Use actual examples, what's been tried, where and how it works. Do your homework, get the word out, create visual representations. Be positive and hopeful.

9. Learn from Your Mistakes

You're gonna make mistakes; we all do. Critique—in a positive way—yourself, the movement, and the opposition. What works, and why? What isn't working? What do people really enjoy doing?—and do more of that.

10. Take Care of Yourself and Each Other

Maintain balance. Eat well and get regular exercise. Avoid burnout by delegating tasks, sharing responsibility, and maintaining an open process. Be sensitive to your comrades. Have fun. As much as possible, surround yourself with others (both at work and at play) who share your vision so you can build camaraderie, solidarity, and support. Enjoy yourself, and nourish your sense of humour. Remember: you're not alone!

So there you have it. Tools for the Evolution. You can easily join the millions of people around the world working towards ecological health and sustainability just by doing something. With a bit of effort, and some extraordinary luck, a sustainable future may be assured for us and the planet. Go forth and agitate.

Tooker Gomberg (1955–2004) was a long-time activist, writer, and former Edmonton City councillor—and an inspiration to everyone who knew him. Angela Bischoff is a tireless worker, activist, author, and co-founder of several organizations, including EcoCity and Greenspiration!

This article originally appeared on the "Greenspiration!" website ‹www.greenspiration.org›.

Additional Resources

For more information on affinity groups, handbooks, and manuals for direct action planning, and for other activist tools
www.stopftaa.org
www.protest.net
www.activist.ca
www.pax.protest.net
www.globalizethis.org
www.ruckus.org/resources/index.html
www.rantcollective.org
www.democracyproject.ca
www.ecawar.org

Or check out local labour, environmental, feminist, anti-poverty, or other social justice groups for direct action training.

Legal support
Activists' Legal Project (UK) · www.activistslegalproject.org.uk
G8 ACT Legal Collective · http://g8.activist.ca/legal/
Legal Support Ottawa · www.flora.org/legal/index.html
Libertas legal collective (Quebec) · (514) 262-4746
Midnight Special Law Collective · www.midnightspecial.net/
National Lawyers Guild (US) · www.nlg.org/
The Just Law Collective · www.lawcollective.org/
The NYC People's Law Collective · www.nycplc.mahost.org
D.C. Justice & Solidarity Collective · www.justiceandsolidarity.org/
Liberty Guide to Human Rights (UK) · www.yourrights.org.uk/

Propaganda tools
www.protest.bmgbiz.net
www.protestposters.org
www.protestgraphics.org
www.guerillagirls.com
www.uhc-collective.org.uk

Get your message out

www.indymedia.org
www.radio4all.org
www.thepetitionsite.com

Media hoaxes

www.theyesmen.org
www.rtmark.com

Radical cheerleaders

www.geocities.com/radicalcheerleaders
http://radcheers.tripod.com/RC/

Critical mass

www.criticalmassrides.info/

Guerrilla gardening

www.primalseeds.org/index.htm
http://primalseeds.nologic.org/guerrillagardening.htm
www.moregardens.org
www.publicspace.ca/gardeners.htm

Culture jamming

www.culturejamming101.com

Boycotts

www.maquilasolidarity.org/tools
www.boycotts.org

PIRGs

www.apirg.org
www.opirg.org
www.sfu.ca/~sfpirg

Field Notes

This book is printed on Rolland Enviro Edition 100 made in Canada by Cascades Fine Papers. It is 100% post-consumer recycled, processed chlorine-free, and ancient forest-friendly.